Peterman Rides Again

PETERMAN RIDES AGAIN

*Adventures Continue with the
Real "J. PETERMAN" through
Life & the Catalog Business*

John Peterman

Prentice
Hall Press

Library of Congress Cataloging-in-Publication Data

Peterman, John.
    Peterman rides again. / John Peterman.
        p. cm.
    ISBN 0-7352-0199-4
    1. Industrial management.   2. Success in business.   3. Entrepreneurship.
I. Title.
HD31.P3838 2000
658—dc21   00-045658
                                                                            CIP

Printed in the United States of America

10 9 8 7 6 5 4 3 2 1

ISBN 0-0-7352-0199-4

ATTENTION: CORPORATIONS AND SCHOOLS

Prentice Hall Press books are available at quantity discounts with
bulk purchase for educational, business, or sales promotional use.
For information, please write to: Prentice Hall, Special Sales,
240 Frisch Court, Paramus, NJ 07652. Please supply: title of book,
ISBN, quantity, how the book will be used, date needed.

 Paramus, NJ 07652

http://www.phdirect.com

———◆———

To the wonderful customers and employees of the original J. Peterman Company, and my wife, Audrey, who was there for us all.

———◆———

My thanks to Regina Maruca and Bill McCullam, whose reporting and writing skills helped make this book possible.

Contents

Peterman Rides Again

Security is mostly a superstition.
Life is either a daring adventure or nothing.

—H. Keller (1880–1968)

Banana Boats,
Cavalry Charges,
and Cowboys

"Ten million dollars," said the fat man with red hair. "We bid ten million dollars for the assets of The J. Peterman Company. " The auctioneer's gavel came down with a sharp Crack! The new owners of what had been my baby were laughing, jumping up and down, slapping each other on the back.

The bankruptcy auction had gone on for 11 hours, in the same hotel ballroom where we used to have our company Christmas parties. People had kept coming up to me, asking "How do you feel, John?"

"Fine," I lied.

I walked across the street to the courthouse to witness the signing of the final papers. Then I had a double bourbon and went home to bed.

———◆———

For the twelve years The J. Peterman Company was in business, we had a great time. We laughed, we argued, we made mistakes, and we had successes. We sold through a catalog, at first, and later on added some retail stores. Our catalogs used watercolors and pen-and-ink sketches instead of photographs, and had long, literate copy—college writing courses actually made them assigned reading. Our stores were like my grandmother's barn, filled with odd and wonderful discoveries, something unique around every corner. Our products came from all over the world, from every culture, ethnic origin, and era. We sold items like the silverware from the House of Commons—the very same knives, forks, and spoons that Churchill, Chamberlain, and Macmillan ate with. We sold shirts from Otavalo in the Ecuadorian Andes. Vintage motorcycles with sidecars. French posters from the 1920s and 1930s. Chinese porcelain salvaged from an 18th-century shipwreck. And of course, the J. Peterman signature product, the horseman's duster.

We considered our customers to be our friends.

The company didn't come into being as the result of some grand, well-thought-out business-school plan. I never sat down and said I want to build *this* kind of organization, with *this* kind of culture, aimed at attracting *that* kind of customer. I knew that I enjoyed working in a place that rewarded creativity and initiative; that was the kind of environment where you could have fun. And I strongly suspected that there was a market for products that were not mainstream—that there were lots of people out there who wanted to be slightly different in a world of sameness. I had always wanted to control my own destiny, but had never really thought about running a business, much less one founded on my own feelings about living life fully, about travel and adventure. Like most things in my life, the company was a combination of dreams, luck, persistence, and hard work.

The J. Peterman Company was born, as it were, with my own purchase of a cowboy duster—a coat that signified everything the company was to become because, for me, it meant being different. It meant cowboy. It meant romance. It meant adventure. The duster wasn't just protection against the rain. I bought it because it satisfied something that was gnawing at me—the need to be free of this world's daily grind, overload of information, false fronts, lack of time to reflect. It made me feel like the inner person I want to be true to—the one the world seems to keep trying to stifle.

And when I founded the company, it was because I thought that the duster would help other people feel the same as I did.

———◆———

It's strange to think of a major part of your life's journey pivoting on a coat, but I suppose that's OK if the coat opens the door to an existence that you've only dreamed about. I first saw the coat in Jackson Hole, Wyoming, at a store called Schaffer Outfitters, run by a fellow named Cub Schaffer. Jackson Hole is an upscale ski resort area in the middle of the Grand Teton National Park, on the western border of Wyoming, about 50 miles south from Yellowstone as the peregrine flies. At the time, in 1986, the town of Jackson wasn't terribly expensive. It was upscale, but it hadn't really been "discovered," like Vail or Aspen. Now it's a different story, but elk still have the right of way in Jackson.

The duster was in the back of the store, hanging on a rack with other coats and jackets. It was cut very long, all the way to the floor, similar to the ones in the 1880s. They had to be long because cowboys wore them for protection from dust, rain, snow, and mud while they were riding their horses. If you were on a horse, you wanted a coat that would cover your legs, something that was really full-length. A real duster drags on the ground when you're standing.

I hadn't been shopping for a duster. But I have always had a fascination with cowboys, and I've counted some of them among my friends. A cowboy doesn't talk much, but when he

4

does, he gets straight to the point and has something to say. He usually has an interesting perspective on life because he's had time to reflect on it; you can't have a perspective if you haven't had time to think about what it might be. And a cowboy's word is his bond; no need for reams of legal papers. There's also *something*—I guess you could use the word romantic—about being alone on the range for long periods of time. You, your horse, and nature. It doesn't get any better. Danger, hardship, and deprivation are faced and dealt with every day with a matter-of-course attitude. Most people waste time and energy on the unnecessary; the cowboy uses his energy to do what is truly necessary at the time—no wasted motion.

Growing up in the 1950s, in West Nyack, New York, a mostly rural town about 25 miles up the Hudson River from New York City, I guess I had the basic perception every kid did at that time of the Old West. Hopalong Cassidy, Gene Autry, Roy Rogers, and the rest of that cast loomed largely in my active fantasy life. (Autry and Rogers were slightly suspect, though, because of all that singing.)

One of my favorite fantasies was (and still is) to participate in a mounted cavalry charge. Wouldn't even have to lead it, just participate in it. First saw it in the movie *She Wore a Yellow Ribbon*, with John Wayne. The U.S. Cavalry versus the Apache Indians. Political correctness had not yet entered into our lives.

5

You line up a hundred horsemen in a straight line. Guns, sabers, flags. Nervous horses, pawing the ground, jigging in place, flared nostrils, ears straight up, 1,300 pounds of muscle just as anxious as you are. It's the middle of August. The ground is hard and dry. Any movement causes dust. One hundred horses cause a lot of dust. It's 7:30 in the morning, but it's already hot and humid, as the South is in August. There's a faint smell of honeysuckle, mixed with the smell of horses and leather. Some of the horses are lathered up because they're nervous; that makes their smell even more intense. You check that your gun and your saber are where you want them. Your feet are where you want them in the stirrups. The reins are firmly in hand, and now let's get on with it. At the signal, the line moves forward, first at the walk, all in unison. Then the order to trot, still in the straight line. Then the canter, a ragged straight line like a storm front breaking. The bugler blows charge, you go into a dead run, the straight line disappears, it's the fastest horses out front now, a rush of fear and exhilaration and no stopping until you engage the enemy. There's no time to review your life or pray—that should have been done earlier.

The coat said something about me that I wanted said. It said that I don't need to wear something with a logo to show people who I am. So I bought it.

I was a consultant in sales management at the time. An independent operator. Essentially, I helped companies with everything from product positioning, pricing, and distribution to motivating sales staff. My expertise came largely through fourteen years in sales management at General Foods and Dole Pineapple, which had been folded into Castle and Cook Foods, and three years as the national sales and marketing manager at International Spike, a start-up company that sold Jobe's plant-fertilizer spikes.

I wasn't scheduled to be in Jackson Hole. The truth was, I'd been in Denver on business, found myself bored and restless, and decided on impulse to go to Wyoming. I'd never been to any of those western ski resort towns, and I was curious.

———◆———

Impulsive actions like that—going to Jackson Hole when I was supposed to be heading someplace else—aren't out of character for me. I've always been impulsive. It's how I'm wired. Once, when I was in my twenties, I hopped a banana boat to Costa Rica. I was working for Dole Pineapple as a sales manager at the time, and also working in a sort of lend-lease capacity as a special marketing consultant for AID, a U.S. government program that lent money to underdeveloped countries so that they could build up their infrastructures. Because I had to go to Costa Rica anyway, I decided it would be more of an adventure if I took a freighter rather than just getting on a plane in Miami. Dole ran banana boats regularly from Gulfport, Mississippi to La Ceiba, Honduras, and Limón, Costa Rica. I called my friend Gino Scaldone, who was the manager of the fresh-fruit shipping operation. He told me when the next boat was leaving and when to be there.

It was late afternoon when I got to the *Asseburg*, a break-bulk freighter of German registry. Black hull, white superstructure, about 550 feet long, with the cabin and stack amidships. She had a crew of 24—12 officers and 12 hands. In those days, Dole shipped its bananas in boxes; today everything goes in containers. Quite frankly, container ships have no romance at all compared with the old break-bulks. Most of the freighters like the *Asseburg* had what was called the owner's cabin, as well as another stateroom or two. There's no room for passengers on today's container ships. Too bad; it's one of the best ways to travel.

I stayed in the owner's cabin on the *Asseburg*. It was next to the captain's cabin, and adjacent to the officers' mess. I had a living room with a sofa, coffee table, bar, and a writing desk under the porthole, a comfortable bedroom with two beds, night tables, and a dresser, plus a small, efficient bath. The ship had been built in Europe, probably in the 1950s, and everything was well made by skilled craftsmen; you couldn't slip a cigarette paper into the seams where mahogany met steel. This was a real owner's cabin, this was a real working freighter, these were real seafaring men. The food was excellent. I remember in particular the ceviche; it was the best I'd ever had or have had to this day. I would sit outside on deck with a drink and watch the sun go down. The weather was warm—not too hot, not too cold, not cloudy; there was a breeze. The briny smell was right, the breeze was right, the sun setting over the ocean was right. Everything was in sync, and it couldn't have gotten any better.

You can always tell how good the helmsman is by how straight the wake is. This one you could see stretching straight back for miles.

As night began to set in, I would be joined by the captain and one or two other officers. Wolfgang Kalish was the captain's name. He wasn't what I expected (everyone seems to have a stereotype of what a ship's captain should look like), but I liked him. He was about 5' 11", wiry, mid-50s, dark hair and bushy eyebrows. Spoke perfect English with an Erich von Stroheim accent. We drank German beer long into the night and told stories. The captain had many more stories than I did at that point. I thought myself quite worldly then, but I really hadn't been anywhere. I was just beginning to connect what I had read about in history and travel books with the real world. I remember asking the captain if he had ever been to the U.S. He looked at me with a smile and said, "Oh, yes, I haff spent some time in Arkansas." Turns out he had been a submariner on a U-boat in WWII; the U-boat was captured on the surface, and he became a prisoner of war. He was taken to a prison camp in the Ozarks.

The entire freighter trip—three days, two nights—cost me $25 per night for room and meals, and $12 for my bar bill. Total, $62. Try that today.

———◆———

I wore the coat out of the store. But I didn't wear it in quite the right way. This duster was constructed with the modern-day cowboy-wannabe in mind; it had snaps all the way around it, at three levels, so that you could, in effect, hem the thing to the length you wanted. And I guess I was feeling a little self-conscious. So I had snapped it up to make it look like a "normal" raincoat, just slightly longer than knee-length.

That lasted about ten minutes. I was wandering around, window shopping, and I stopped when I caught sight of my reflection. I was disappointed at what I saw. I had bought the coat because it was long; it went all the way to the ground. I thought, "Why did I buy this if I was going to snap it up to look like something it isn't?" I unsnapped it, and felt like I was at last my own person. I was different, and I didn't care. In fact, I liked it.

I wore the duster all the time after that. I wore it to New York City on business trips. I wore it to San Francisco. London. The local grocery store.

Everybody liked the duster. Once, when I was at the Atlanta airport, in from San Francisco, trying to catch the last plane home to Lexington, Kentucky, I was almost pulled down by a guy who grabbed my coattails as I ran by. He was in his late 40s, built like an ex-linebacker who'd kept on eating and drinking the way he had in his playing days. Business suit, wrinkled white shirt, loosened necktie. As I spun around, I could see a couple of miniature Jack Daniels in his shirt pocket. "Grrreat coat," he slurred, weaving into my face, both of us off balance. "Where I can get one a' them?"

People also seemed to like *me*—people who didn't even know me—just because I was wearing the duster. I think the coat said the same thing to them that it said to me; they, too, wanted to be their own person. The fact that a floor-length, off-white canvas coat tends to stand out didn't hurt, either. Within a few weeks, someone who knew me well, Donald Staley, actually came out and said it: "You know, Peterman, I like you better because you're wearing that coat."

Don was a long-time friend, a brilliant creative thinker and copywriter; he sees through the clutter around ideas, spots opportunities, and exploits them with the kind of unexpected communications that people haven't had a chance to develop an immunity to.

We'd worked on many projects together. Once, in the mid-eighties, before The J. Peterman Company, we pitched the State of Kentucky tourism department for the advertising agency job. There had just been an election; there was a new governor and new top-level political appointments. Through some friends of mine we had good contacts all the way up to the governor's office. Don and I got an appointment with the new guys who had just come into office in the tourism department. We gave a great presentation, fresh ideas—Don had serious experience writing for travel and tourism accounts. Well, we landed the job. Then reality set in when the people at the incumbent agency in Louisville found out and pulled some strings of their own. We were fired within 24 hours of winning the business. I found it amusing, really. Sometimes I still imagine how the look on the new director of tourism's face must have changed when he announced that he had hired some outsiders and smacked right into the reality of state politics.

At any rate, I remember clearly the moment Don told me he liked me better in the duster. It was early December, 1986, and I had just walked into his apartment on New York's Upper East Side, where he did his copywriting and consulting. The entrance hallway had a table piled with all sorts of men's hats. A Sherlock Holmes deerstalker, a collapsible opera hat, a wide-brimmed fur felt Borsalino, a real Montecristi panama woven so tightly it could hold water without leaking—maybe 20 hats in all. The rooms beyond were shadowy, with pools of warm light from table lamps illuminating other odd collections. The walls were lined with imposing bookcases. There was a picture or two that Don had done when he was painting, years before. He had started his creative career as an artist; however, he discovered early on that his paintings didn't sell unless he wrote something—a phrase, a caption—at the bottom. He quickly came to realize that he was a much better copywriter than painter.

Don was standing there, wearing his usual oversized shirt, baggy pants and big, clunky leather shoes. He's about 5' 10" tall, 200 pounds, and has always had a full, bushy beard and short hair, cut close and brushed forward, like Caesar's.

I was facing him, briefcase in one hand, suitcase in the other, wearing my duster, cowboy hat, cowboy boots, and jeans. And I said something like, "Yeah, I've noticed that a lot of people seem to like me better when I'm wearing this, even people who don't even know me. If we could sell these things, we could make some money."

———◆———

That was the beginning. But at that moment, there was no thought of building a company around the coat. The idea was that we could sell a few, make a few thousand dollars, and then move on. We decided to run some ads and see what happened. Don would write the copy, describing how I felt when I was wearing the duster, and I would buy the coats and set up some way to take orders and do all the other things I knew absolutely nothing about that would be necessary to run a business. Our first ad was in the Lexington, Kentucky, *Herald Leader*, with a black-and-white drawing of a horseman wearing a duster:

> *The J. Peterman Coat.*
> *$170*
> *Protection against the winds of Wyoming, the blizzards of Wall Street. Classic horseman's duster protects you, your rump, your saddle, and your legs down to the ankles. Because it's cut very long to do the job, it's unintentionally very flattering, with or without a horse. High-count natural cotton canvas. Lightweight waterproof lining. Nine pockets. The first time people see you wearing The J. Peterman Coat, they're going to say, "Where did you get it? I've always wanted one of those." Tell them somewhere east of Laramie.*

Men's and women's sizes XXS, XS, S, M, L, XL, XXL.

Include height and weight when you order. I'll advise best size. Although I live in horse country, I wear this coat for other reasons. Because they don't make Duesenbergs any more.

J. Peterman.

We sold one duster. To my accountant's secretary, so it didn't really count. But, we thought, well, we'll just try one more time. So we ran some more ads, searching for the people we thought might be out there. We also tried some unorthodox marketing. One night, I enlisted the help of a friend of mine, Cotton Nash. Cotton was a three-time All-American basketball player at the University of Kentucky, as well as a professional basketball and baseball player. Although we never played against or with each other during our professional baseball careers, we shared many of the same experiences. Cotton is 6' 7", an imposing figure. We put on our cowboy hats, boots, and dusters and proceeded to try to drum up some interest in most of the bars in Lexington. I don't believe that we sold any dusters that night, but we did show the colors and managed to get gloriously drunk. As I say, we really weren't thinking "build an enterprise" at the time.

(That was in February, 1987. Six months later, Cotton became one of the two initial investors in the company.)

In February, March, and April of that year, I personally sold dusters at some regional craft shows, and at the Rolex Three-Day Event. We also continued to run advertising, with increasing success. We sold about $2,000 worth in February. $5,000 in March. $15,000 in April. Most of the April sales came from our first national ad, which ran in the *New Yorker* magazine. We sold 70 coats with that one advertisement, and The J. Peterman Company was officially up and running.

We brought in $580,000 that year, all from space ads in newspapers and magazines. The experience was exciting, but also terrifying. We were buying small batches of dusters on 30-day terms at wholesale prices. We'd secure the ad space and use the money from our sales to pay for the ad, but then we had to run another ad to get the money to pay for the dusters, and the cycle kept repeating. I soon owed so much money, I couldn't have gotten out of the business if I'd wanted to. It was like the opening scene in *Raiders of the Lost Ark*, where Harrison Ford is being chased by the giant rolling boulder.

———◆———

The J. Peterman Company—and the Owner's Manual, as we called the catalog through which we soon began to sell our goods—introduced the Peterman persona to millions. (The *Seinfeld* television series, which regularly featured a

"J. Peterman" character, later brought more name recognition.) At its peak, the Owner's Manual had a circulation of 18 million. We mailed it to customers in the U.S., Japan, Russia—countries all over the world. We sold thousands of different items during the life of the company, though the duster remained our signature product. Eventually, we moved beyond the catalog business and opened stores in Grand Central Station, San Francisco, and Seattle, among other places. We soared in the early 1990s. The company had gained a momentum of its own. It was a fun place to work, an exciting place to be. Then it stumbled, and fell. Hard.

But I'm getting ahead of myself. If I'm going to tell the story of my company, I should go back to the beginning and give you some context. And I should also clarify some things. The J. Peterman Company is a big part of this book. But the story of the company's rise and fall isn't the only reason I'm sitting down to write.

This book is about the adventures and experiences that enabled me to start The J. Peterman Company in the first place. It's about the lessons I learned during its life, and how they've made me capable of starting, and, hopefully, succeeding at, whatever I choose to do next. Sharing those things might be helpful to a person who's thinking of starting a business, who's actually running one, or is just interested in what makes the world tick.

This book is about dreaming and doing, about the ability to let yourself dream and then make those dreams come true. It's about having an imagination and using it. It's about taking risks and not being afraid to fail, even when you've failed before. It's about the subtle and not-so-subtle ways others influence our lives, sifting out the positives and pushing back the negatives in order to cut your own path, despite difficulties and criticism. It's about working hard, planning, and executing, again and again, developing a sincere attitude of excitement about what will happen next rather than having a sense of fear, dread, or anxiety about the future. I haven't seen it all, or done it all, but a lot has gone on in my life. And these days I get up in the morning and say, "Damn, I can't wait to see what's going to happen today."

There's a hard-boiled view of business out there—that business is unemotional, or should be unemotional. I don't buy that. I don't believe you can create a business without passion. I believe, in fact, that creating a business should be a great love affair. In order to create something from nothing, you need to have a passion about what you're doing. Passion fuels action, action leads to learning, and the three together lead to success.

Although the trademark "J. Peterman" still exists, I have no association with it. Nor, as far as I can tell, does it represent the tenets it originally did. Paul Harris Stores bought the company and the rights to the J. Peterman name at the bank-ruptcy auction.

The spark that started the company is still a part of me, though. And I still wear the duster all the time.

Dreams come true; without that possibility, nature would not incite us to have them.

—J. Updike (1932–   )

Dreaming
and Doing

I'm riding Waldo, my Quarter horse, the fastest breed on Earth over a quarter-mile. We're not fully acquainted with each other yet, but there's one thing we agree on—we both love to run. It's a cool spring day, a rush of moist air that smells of wet earth and new grass, my duster is streaming out behind me . . .

Without warning, Waldo breaks hard to the left, spooked by something, maybe a shadow cast by a cloud. I continue straight on over his head in a textbook demonstration of Newton's First Law. The rider behind me canters up for damage inspection and finds nothing serious. "That's one of the damnedest things I ever saw," he says. "You looked like a giant white bat."

I'm on my rump in the mud, dizzy but laughing. I'm still very happy about being out there, riding a horse.

My own horse.

You have to go back to your childhood, I think, to find where your most important dreams had their beginnings. What fascinated you then? What did you spend hours thinking about, creating scenes in your mind and replaying them? What did you like to draw on brown paper with Crayolas or sketch on the inside covers of your schoolbooks?

Those aren't idle questions. As a child, you're exposed to a rapidly expanding universe of images, ideas, people, but only certain things hold special fascination. If you stayed in touch with them, they may already have developed into driving forces that have moved you to a life that feels satisfying, right, fully lived. And if you haven't stayed in touch, the good news is that it's never too late to reclaim them.

There were farms and horses all around when I was growing up. During summer vacation, my friends and I used to sneak rides on the horses that were boarding at a neighboring farm. Jimmy and Neil would muster at my house after breakfast and we'd cross the road, skirt the evergreens at the top of Robinson's land, cut up behind Ogden's goat farm into the hardwood forest, climb down into the gorge, traverse the brook at a place we called Big Rock, go up the other side of the gorge, snake through two big abandoned pastures overgrown with sage grass and blackberry brambles, and walk about a half mile through the birch woods, emerging at the old Dutch stone wall that marked the top of the horse pasture. A mile-and-a-half expedition in all; you had to really want to make it.

The horses were reluctant participants in our game at first, and coy most days after that; we had to work for our rides. It took a half hour or so just to get close to a horse. I remember trying to sneak up from behind, and finding out quickly that it wasn't a good plan—the horse would startle and bolt, or worse. If the horse could see me coming, I had a much better chance at a ride. And I soon figured out that if I brought an apple or a carrot or two, my chances increased exponentially.

We weren't very tall; the horses seemed huge. We had to lead them to a place where there was a log or a big stone in order to be able to mount. No saddles, of course. Occasionally, a horse would have a halter on, and then we would use lengths of clothesline we'd brought along as makeshift reins. Usually, though, they were just there in their natural horse state and so we'd climb on and they would do exactly as they pleased. We had no idea how to make rope halters, and we lacked the courage to go into the barn and commandeer tack—not that we would have known what to do with it if we had.

Sometimes the horses kept grazing, not minding us fly-weights sitting on top. Sometimes they would try to brush us off by walking under the low branches of the trees along the fence line, or wander over to the run-in shed and just stand around socializing with each other. When we'd catch one in the upper pasture, it would often take off running down the sloping hill through the gaps in the stone walls dividing the pastures to the barn at the bottom. I jumped off the first few times when a horse I'd managed to mount started to run. Later on, the running was what I wanted.

I don't know whether Jimmy and Neil loved riding those horses as much as I did. I doubt it. For me, though, I knew the first time I got up close to a horse that it was important for me to own one, someday.

When you're a child you can't simply say, "This is my dream, now I'm going to make it come true," and then go out and do so. You haven't got the freedom, the resources, or the understanding of how the world works. I knew that I wanted to own a horse—that dream was clear—but I didn't buy Waldo until I was 46.

What happens instead is that you keep on thinking about and coveting the things that fascinate you. Your eyes and ears seek out reminders of them without your even trying; if your fascination with horses is strong, you'll walk down a street and just happen to notice, on the far wall inside that barber shop over there, a framed photograph of Man O' War. And eventually, when the world begins to allow you more choices, you'll start making the ones that lead you in the direction of your dreams. Given two available summer jobs, one at a stable and another at the local ice cream shop, you pick the stable. A relatively small choice, not really proactive, but it may lead to becoming a jockey, a stable owner, a veterinarian—or moving to Kentucky.

I had another clear dream as a child: from the age of nine or ten, I wanted to play major league baseball. As I moved through little league, high school ball, and summer leagues to college ball, I consciously made decisions that led me closer to the prize. They weren't hard decisions to make, though some may have seemed illogical to other people. Like playing in two leagues during the summers, instead of going to the beach with my friends. And dropping out of NROTC at the end of my sophomore year at Holy Cross, so that I could play right after college. That raised eyebrows, but to me it seemed the most natural thing in the world.

I'd hit a respectable .275 in varsity baseball that year, good enough to convince me that I had a shot at the majors. So even though I knew that my resumé would have looked better with "Naval Officer" on it than "Third Baseman" (this was before baseball meant Big Money), I went to the NROTC officer to resign.

The commanding officer was sitting ramrod straight in his chair and looking at me with disapproval. He had a gruff, jowly military presence, like Sterling Hayden in *Doctor Strangelove*, and he inclined his head as he looked at me, making it seem as if he were looking down at me even though we were at eye level with each other. "I haven't heard that you're that good," he said, shaking his head. "And even if you get as far as the minors, you'll never make any money. You know, in the minors, they pay you with a sack of potatoes."

I remember thinking, "This guy is a real old timer. Potatoes?" but not saying anything. Then he shuffled some papers and dismissed me with a nod. As I stood up to leave, he delivered the parting shot. "You wouldn't have made a very good naval officer anyway, Peterman." I didn't look back.

That was the first time I had ever really gone against the wishes of an adult authority figure. I had actually expected him to be supportive of my decision, as grown-ups had usually been about decisions I'd made. It was a dose of reality, and it occurred to me that I'd been very fortunate not to have met too many people like him.

———◆———

You may have encountered the equivalent of that NROTC officer much earlier on. An awful lot of adults stifle children's dreams, and thus, their potentially satisfying futures. Maybe your parents, caretakers, or teachers want you to behave in a certain kind of way so that you won't be a nuisance to them as they go about their busy lives. Maybe your interests are enough left of center that you'd be considered a bit odd, an embarrassment to them. "Why can't you behave more like Jack, or Jenny?" Did you hear something like that at one time or another?

I'm willing to acknowledge that many adults don't consciously know they're pouring cement on top of a young seedling. They may be genuinely thinking of a child's best interests. But the repressive result is the same as if they had done it on purpose. Because most children want to please the adults they depend on for almost everything, they'll take the criticisms into their hearts and keep repeating them. "I can't do that" and "I should do this" become automatic responses that seem to come from you, yourself, and seem to be perfectly sensible.

When I began fantasizing about being a major-league baseball player, I was maybe four feet tall, with skinny little arms and skinny little legs. The guy I was dreaming about being? His wrist was bigger than my waist. But nobody pointed that out. I was lucky. My mother and dad were always encouraging. In fact, my dad organized the building of the first backstop we had at our little-league practice field, when I was ten.

The field was a level spot on what had once been an extensive sand quarry. They had struck water and abandoned the project years before; the flooded sand pit became our swimming hole, and the rest of the site was our playing field. We'd play baseball with as few as two or three on a side, making up rules to fit the situation. If there was no left-fielder, it was an automatic out when you hit into left. It was an automatic home run, always, if you hit into the swamp in deep right. We played with baseballs that had long since lost their covers and were held together with black electrician's tape. We always had a couple of them, but without a backstop it was still often a long time between pitches.

My dad convened a "work party"—whenever there was a community project in our neighborhood, they called it a work party—and he and I and volunteers from six or seven other families worked a long Saturday putting up the backstop, with six-by-six square posts sunk into the ground to make a structure angled like a fireplace, wide in front, narrow in back. Dad wore an old blue shirt with the sleeves rolled up, the sweat running down his neck, soaking the collar, as he used the posthole digger. We mixed concrete and poured it into the holes to anchor the posts. Then we stretched two rows of fence wire around them, one on top of the other, so it went up about eight feet, and nailed boards over the fencing behind home plate.

My dad took me to major-league games whenever he could. The Brooklyn Dodgers at Ebbets Field, the Giants at the Polo Grounds, and the Yankees, of course, at Yankee Stadium. Baseball was important then. In high school, they would put televisions in the cafeteria and the study halls when the World Series games were on, and announce scores over the PA system.

I saw my first live game at Ebbets Field, with PeeWee Reese, Duke Snyder, Roy Campanella, and Jackie Robinson. I remember the thrill I felt when they played the national anthem, a sense that something very important was happening. Eventually, I decided that the Yankees did the anthem best. Players on the other teams would stand where their positions were for the anthem, but the Yankees would be in groups of two, the pitcher with the catcher, the second baseman with the shortstop; it seemed to have some kind of solemn significance. I also remember being taken aback by how red the dirt was on the baseline and the warning track at Yankee Stadium. It was red because they mixed regular dirt with brick dust, my dad explained, and the Yankees used more brick dust than anyone else.

Dad came to every game he could when I played little league. My mother would pick him up at the train station after his day at work in Manhattan and they would both come straight to the field. They'd see the last couple of innings, and then we'd climb into our DeSoto four-door and go home for supper. In the car, dad would ask me about the parts of the game he'd missed, tell me "That was a great catch" or some such comment on what he'd seen, we'd talk about the hits I got. Nothing critical, even if I'd bombed.

I still have a black-and-white photo of me when I was 19, sliding into home plate during a summer-league game. My dad is standing at the fence on the third base side, leaning way to his right, sliding into home with me, his concentration as intense as mine.

———◆———

When you're allowed to pursue a dream, making choices that keep you true to it, and you hit a point where it starts to come true, it feels both amazingly vivid and perfectly natural at the same time.

My workout at Yankee Stadium was like that. I had just returned from the College World Series in Omaha, where I went 2 for 10 and made a couple of errors. A terrible series. Still, I had hit over .300 my last two years in college and done really well in the Series the year before, hitting over .400.

I'd had conversations with scouts from the Baltimore Orioles, Houston Astros, and Pittsburgh Pirates, who had seen me play all through college. I don't remember ever talking to a Yankee scout. And then, out of the blue, the Yankees gave me a call. On Wednesday, June 19, 1963, I found myself in the locker room at Yankee Stadium, off in an alcove they must have reserved for prospects like me—wall-to-wall carpeting, lockers that didn't have doors on them. I got a look at the main locker room where the team dressed, the trainer's room, with a whirlpool and a rub-down table, and another room where a big table was covered with hundreds of baseballs. The players would autograph a quota of balls each day; this was before they started charging for signed baseballs.

As I was reaching into my locker to pull out the Yankee uniform, Ralph Houk walked up. A tall gent with the presence and bearing of a Marine Corps major, which he was, dressed in a perfectly tailored sharkskin suit. "Hi, John, my name is Ralph Houk," he said, as if I didn't know who he was. "Glad to have you here. As soon as you're ready, Frank Crosetti will hit you some infield, and then you can take batting practice."

It was the first time I'd ever been on a major-league field. The dirt seemed even more red than I remembered, the grass bright green in contrast. The stands surrounding the field like a wall seemed to rise up for a mile. The sky was very far away. The ghosts of Ruth and Gehrig were very close. And the place echoed. Every crack of a bat reverberated.

Crosetti told me to go on out to second base and began hitting grounders to me with a fungo bat, first directly at me, then to my right and left. He hit precisely one foot further out each time, testing my range; how far could I go? It was uncanny how accurately he could place the ball. When he got to the outer limits, I began to cheat. As he tossed the ball into the air, I would break one way or the other; he would inevitably hit in the opposite direction.

When it came time for me to hit, Crosetti told me to get a bat and come back to the batting cage. I grabbed one out of the rack, weighing it in my hand. Not too heavy, not too light; the handle felt just right. Baseball bats are not created equal. If the grain is close together, the surface is hard and you have more control over where the ball goes; if it's wide, the bat will start to flake on contact. A straight grain makes for a stronger bat. The balance between the barrel and the handle is critical to delivering maximum force to the ball. I started to turn, then heard a low growl. "That's my bat, put it back, rookie." It was Elston Howard. A serious growl, but both he and Yogi were smiling. I looked at the bat again, saw the number 32 on the end. Aha, find one without a number. I *knew* that. I grabbed an unmarked one, and ran up to the cage.

There I was, standing next to Roger Maris, Joe Pepitone, Whitey Ford. And it fit. *I* fit. (Mickey Mantle had caught his foot under the fence in Baltimore the day before, and Bobby Richardson's father had died, so they missed their chance to witness my performance.) Maris stepped in and knocked eight or ten balls into the right field bleachers. "OK, Peterman, jump in," Crosetti said.

Maris and I both hit left-handed. All similarity ended there.

The first pitch took forever to get to the plate. I had no blood in my veins at that point, just adrenaline. I swung and missed. "OK," I said to myself, "just hit the ball." Next pitch, I smacked it to deep right field, high and far. I watched it go and thought, "Maybe upper deck," then, "Well, at least lower deck," then, "The warning track, maybe." Somebody shagged my ball in front of the warning track.

I reassessed my 160-pound frame. "Line drives over the infield," I told myself, "that's what got you here."

After the workout, Maris spent some time with me in the clubhouse, telling me which minor-league towns were the best. I showered, changed, and went upstairs to the Stadium Club. Johnny Johnson, head of the Yankee minor-league system, was waiting for me. I'd had a good workout, he said, and they were interested in me. How much did I want?

This was before agents; you did your own deals. I was already talking to some other clubs. I knew the Yankees always had the most and best talent in their system, so if I was going to sign with them, I wanted to make sure they were really interested. "Well, I've been offered $10,000," I said. "I think that's a good number, and I really like the Yankees." Johnson gave me a straight look. "You ought to take that offer; we don't think you're worth that much."

I signed with the Pirates a few days later. For, let's just say, less than $10,000.

My three-year career with the Pirates looked like a pyramid. Class A to AAA, back down to Class A, and exit. I had highs that I couldn't have conceived of. Leading the league in hitting for two months and making the All-Star team in my first year. Spring training with Roberto Clemente. Playing with and against guys with real talent. I also had lows, like the time I broke my leg during a game in Florida. I woke up two days later in a hospital bed, with friends, fellow players, and their girlfriends having a party in my room, waiting for me to join in. I was groggy and nauseous. Someone handed me a beer; fortunately, my hands weren't working right, and most of it went down my hospital gown.

I was privileged to be involved in a classic baseball fight with Reggie Smith, who wound up playing right field for the Los Angeles Dodgers and had a great career. Reggie put his feet up while sliding into second base and spiked me in the shoulder, so I bounced the ball off his head. We called each other names, pushed and shoved each other, and then everybody was there, pulling us apart. A necessary but harmless testosterone display.

All of us then were in the game because we had a passion for it, and that made even the smallest details of life on a farm team exciting. It was *Bull Durham* without the candles. All those little stadiums—Batavia, New York; Kingsport,

Tennessee; Harlan, Kentucky; Bluefield, West Virginia. Infields with rocks the size of your fist and lights that only sometimes worked, but that's the way it was. Living for days on hot dogs and candy bars. Riding all night from game to game over mountain roads in old buses with rounded backs and no rear windows. And the girls who would hang out during the games. They would give the batboys notes to take to us in the dugout. The batboy would come up to you, hand you a note, and say, "It's the girl in the eighth row. She wants to talk to you after." And you'd look, and she'd look away, and then look back, and smile.

———◆———

When you pursue a dream with limited resources and aren't really generating your options on your own, you may find it seems to be within your grasp only to have it slip through your fingers. That was true of me and professional baseball. I always suspected that my size might hold me back, and I certainly couldn't start a team of my own. That broken leg slowed me way down, too.

The J. Peterman Company was, for a period of years, quite another matter. Once the hard initial work was done, all sorts of resources began to fall into place. We created our own choices. Obstacles seemed to melt away, and the operation took on a kind of natural flow. A key reason for the difference may well have been that the company was driven by more than one dream—my desire for independence, yes, and fascination with horses and the West, but also a childhood dream of being a world traveler, of going to remote places and bringing back treasure.

From the time I was eight or nine until well into my teens, I used to sit up in our attic on rainy days and evenings and pore over *National Geographic* magazines. My parents kept stacks of them there, going back for decades. I would take two or three at a time, settle into a space I'd made for myself between boxes and stored furniture under a light bulb with a string pull, and go far away for hours, until I was summoned back, and down, to dinner.

The paper stock was thick and glossy, and the printing ink had a sharp, pleasantly chemical smell. The maps were menus filled with tantalizing choices . . . Rangoon, Ulan Bator, Kuala Lumpur, Karakoram, the Great Eastern Erg. I well remember an article on the ladies of Bali, photographed by the fortunate M.O. Williams, and another, equally stirring in its own way, that took me along the Silk Road with Marco Polo. I was there when Hiram Bingham stumbled up from the jungle to discover Machu Picchu, and when Howard Carter shined his flashlight into Tutankhamen's tomb:

"Can you see anything?"

"Yes, wonderful things."

Could someone who had never read those magazines and dreamed of being an explorer go on to start a company that sought out the best the whole world has to offer? Absolutely. That's just the sort of scheme that a clever MBA might come up with in what's been called "the experience economy." But I doubt that the MBA would bring the same energy to the job, and I doubt that he'd find it so satisfying.

———————◆———————

The Irrawaddy is wide and meanders through a broad, flat plain from which its banks slope down very gradually. It's quiet on the river. A few steam- and diesel-powered boats, but no jet-skis or outboard motors.

I'm on the Road to Mandalay, *a modern yacht run by the people who operate the Orient Express. It was designed for 120 passengers; there are 20 of us on board.*

Last night was "longi" night. I wore the mandatory Burmese male garb with my white dinner jacket. Ian improvised jazz on the piano. We drank cognac and listened to the music, leaning back in rattan lounge chairs under the stars.

This evening will be less demanding. I'm sitting on the observation deck, making a rectangular frame with my hands, peering through it to view a slowly unrolling scroll of golden temples and little fishing villages where life is still much the same as it was a thousand years ago. The boat changes course slightly. The sun sinks a notch closer to the horizon. Light flares unexpectedly off the domes of the pagodas. Bedazzled again.

———◆———

How do you go about getting in touch again with your dreams? The first step, I suspect, is to reach way down and try to recall what you used to want, no matter how childish it seems. Do the best you can to ignore that internal censor ("I can't," "I should"); maybe telling yourself this is an experiment will help. And stay away from people who don't support you.

Flip through old photo albums, yearbooks, diaries, and try to remember. Before you go to bed at night, sit down and sincerely ask yourself, inside, what you want; there may be an answer waiting for you some morning. Watch what catches your eye as you move through your day; what would it be like to have that, or be who that is? When you get some hints, it can be helpful to start a file with pictures of things that seem to interest you. If it's beach houses, cut out and save pictures of beach houses, deck furniture, seashells. If it's farmland, save pictures of farms.

As your desire starts to build, make a real choice or two that brings you closer to the object in question. Reality is the most wonderful kind of computer there is; every time you make a choice it's like asking a question that opens up new opportunities. Who knows exactly where they'll lead?

I certainly didn't when I bought that duster in Jackson Hole, Wyoming.

———◆———

Whatever you believe you can do, begin it.
Action has magic, power, and grace to it.

—J. W. von Goethe (1749–1832)

———◆———

Cheese Downstairs
and Dusters Upstairs

It was a cold day on the wrong side of the tracks in Lexington, and I was sitting on a bare plank floor cutting a duster apart, trying to stay warm. The company that supplied me with dusters couldn't keep up with the increasing orders I was placing; I had to figure out how the coat was made and see if I could get the manufacturing done myself. Little piles of brass snaps, stacks of pockets and canvas panels here, corduroy collar over there . . .

Knock at the door. A young man stuck his head in, accompanied by a whiff of cheddar and beer. "Mister Peterman? That new automatic packaging machine you bought is throwing cheese all over the walls."

Entrepreneurship has its moments.

Selling dusters through The J. Peterman Company wasn't the only business I was involved in at the time. Like many people who've dreamed of being independent, I was pursuing a number of ventures simultaneously, in the hope that one of them might really take off and that, meanwhile, I could cover the family expenses.

———◆———

Back in 1982 I had hung out my shingle as a consultant—to anybody, on any topic—and was slightly amazed when people actually started to come to me for advice. The business eventually evolved into a consultancy focused on specialty foods, in the same way that most everything else I've done in my business career has evolved. I have a vision that I need to be in business, or to make money, or to start something, but I'm not quite sure what it's going to look like. So I just start doing it, and I learn as I go along, and then it comes into focus.

(It's a pattern. I hate it that anything about me could be called a pattern.)

That same year, I also bought a 50% interest in a product called Hall's Beercheese. There was a Hall's Restaurant on the Kentucky River about 12 miles outside Lexington, where Hall's Beercheese was first created and proudly served. They'd developed a secret recipe for a creamy, tangy blend of cheddar mixed with Fall City lager and spices, including red pepper, not to be confused with your classic, Limburgerpungent Bierkäse. At the restaurant, they used to put it on the tables at the beginning of the meal with celery, instead of the usual rolls and butter. It was popular and, eventually, the owner of the restaurant, Steve Hall, decided to sell it in supermarkets. That's when I got into the cheese game.

Steve and I bought out another local cheese company called Sara Neal, located in a 1930s brick building on Midland Avenue in a rundown area near the train tracks that had optimistically been designated an "enterprise zone." We didn't buy the business for their cheese—we stopped making that immediately. We bought it for the building and the set-up.

The building had plenty of Depression-era industrial character. Just inside the main door you stepped down to a concrete floor where a mysterious old safe left by the previous tenants presided on one side. Before we moved The J. Peterman Company to a bigger location on Palumbo Drive, in a better part of town, I had a local safecracker come in. He arrived with a team of two apprentices, and they sweated and grunted and swore for about an hour before they got the thing open. Sorry, no forgotten money or historic artifacts inside, not even a matchbook cover. I felt like Geraldo in Al Capone's vault.

The cheese-making room was on that first level. Two large stainless-steel mixers and a couple of packaging machines, battleship-gray walls, bricked-up windows, but it was clean and cool; it actually suited cheese making quite well. Behind that room was a storage cooler, then the loading dock. I hired a former Hall's waitress named Jean to mix the cheese and an eighteen-year-old named Doug to handle packaging and shipping; later, he worked at The J. Peterman Company as our warehouse manager. Orders came in for two or three hundred cases at a time, Jean would mix the cheese, Doug would ship it out, and our specialty foods distributor, Wine and Schulz, would take care of the rest. It was a business that pretty much ran itself.

I spent most of my time upstairs, in one of two large rooms with unfinished floors and wood-printed vinyl paneling on the walls; the other room eventually became the first warehouse for The J. Peterman Company. Two desks, a potbellied stove to supplement the temperamental heating system, bookcases along one wall for my library. The bathroom was tiny and barely functional, and the bathroom door had a mischievous habit of opening by itself, despite a hook lock on the inside. Through my office window (metal mullions, hardened, chipping putty) I had an excellent view of the Midland Avenue gravel works.

I wasn't making much money, at first. People outside central Kentucky don't seem to be all that fond of Hall's Beercheese. The consulting business did better—it brought in $19,000 the first year and a lot more after that—but even though I was good at it I never really enjoyed it. The whole point of consulting is that you're getting other people to effect change. If you do your job right, you work your way out of the job as quickly as you can. You never have the satisfaction of building something you can point to and call your own. And so, in between cheese and advice, I pursued a line of business experiments that eventually led to selling dusters.

One experiment that got considerable attention was the grandly named National Houseplant Diagnostic Laboratory. As sales manager for Jobe's Fertilizer Spikes, I had learned a lot about what makes houseplants grow or not grow, and I also knew the market. Most households have houseplants— Americans were spending well over a billion dollars a year on them at the time—and their owners are often quite attached to them. When their green friends inexplicably begin to droop and shrivel, as they frequently do, people feel a sense of personal failure. If I could solve this problem, I might have a business. And so, I ran a full-page advertisement, written by Don Staley, in *The New York Times*:

> *Send us your weak, your weary, your blotched, your mysteriously yellowing plant leaves. We'll tell you how to cure your plants. Cost: $6.85.*

About 350 hopeful souls mailed in sample leaves for a three-page computerized analysis with advice on reviving the plants, and the offbeat story caught the media's interest. We got a writeup in the *Wall Street Journal*. I was interviewed on radio stations across the country. I even wound up on *Good Morning America* with Joan Lunden and David Hartman. "You mean you want *me*?" I said when they called. They did. Paid my way to New York and put me up in the St. Moritz, overlooking Central Park. Early next morning I dressed in a suit and tie because I thought I should look like a doctor—probably the last time I wore a suit and tie to any business-related event—and was whisked off to the studio in a big black limo. A burly fellow designated to be my "handler" led me into a room supplied with coffee and an impressive carbohydrate array, then on to makeup, where I sat down across from a far more casually attired gent with an entourage buzzing around him. We eyed each other. Finally, he said, "Hi, my name is Tommy Lee Jones. I do movies." "My name is John Peterman," I replied. "I'm a houseplant doctor." We didn't speak again after that.

The houseplant business withered, but instructively. A paid response of 350 wasn't bad, but not nearly enough to recoup the $10,000 it cost to run a page in the *Times*, let alone show a profit. We should have offered some kind of prescriptive plant-care products and equipment as a follow-through with the printed analyses; there would have been no additional advertising expense, and someone who has just bought from you is an ideal prospect for another sale. Unfortunately, a good product line would have required more capital—and I knew nothing about venture capital then.

———◆———

Enter the duster. At first, in mid-1987, it was just me and Don Staley, writing copy for the ads, and Audrey, my wife, whom I enlisted to keep the books, take orders, and handle shipping; she went on to build what some people have called the best customer-service department in the business. Audrey's father, Al, was a retired UPS truck driver, and he helped out with shipping. Because of him, we got UPS to provide lots of service we probably couldn't have extracted from them otherwise. Don stayed in New York, drawing a small salary. Audrey sat at the desk across from mine, in the office over the cheese-making room. She was paid as well—underpaid, but paid.

I didn't take any money, to begin with, and I did everything else during that first year. I started figuring out how to find products for The J. Peterman Company, source products, make products, create the systems we needed. I also talked to customers. Happy ones, unhappy ones. We never let a customer be unhappy for long. We always made things right. Later on, when the company was larger, the joke was to "keep John off the phone." They said I used to give too much stuff away. But we all put the customer first. That was at the core of how I wanted the company run. My feeling was, if customers were unhappy with a product, don't even make them send it back. "Don't bother to return it," I'd tell them, "we'll just send you another" in whatever size or color they wanted.

I knew that policy was a bit liberal, and unrealistic in the long run, but it set the tone that I wanted my company to be true to.

I was constantly testing magazines and newspapers, too, looking for the best returns on our space ads. We would run up to $50,000 worth of ads in a month, in different publications. If the ads didn't pull, the company would have been gone. Ultimately, we tested about thirty or forty different publications and began to develop an expertise in small-space print marketing. The main thing we learned was that it didn't matter how attractive the demographics of a magazine were if it didn't have other mail-order items advertised repeatedly in it; that indicated it had enough readers who were used to ordering through the mail—many people aren't—to make it a worthwhile medium. The *New Yorker* was our best vehicle. The *Smithsonian* and *The New York Times Sunday Magazine* were also good. Early on, Don and I began monitoring where Banana Republic was running ads, assuming that such well-established marketers must know what they were doing. Years later we found out that they were simultaneously watching our ads, as if we possessed The Secret Wisdom of Mail Order.

One of our most spectacular mistakes in those first few months was buying ad space in the United Airlines inflight magazine. It seemed like fish in a barrel—a captive audience that fit perfectly the demographics we had imagined as our target. We had to buy two ads to get in, at $12,000 each, but I thought, "How can we go wrong?" Well, the first ad, which ran in September of 1987, was a disaster. We got three orders out of it. Then we had to sit there, knowing that the second $12,000 was going to go down the tubes, powerless to stop it. It was the most money we had paid for an ad so far. We almost went belly-up right then. In hindsight, our customers were probably on the plane, all right, but they didn't have their noses in the in-flight magazines; more likely they were working, dozing, or reading John Grisham paperbacks.

We were always on the verge of shutting down. I had everything I owned hocked to the hilt. There was very little margin for error. From time to time I would marvel at the risks we were taking. Usually I ended those mental journeys with the thought that since I didn't have very much to begin with, I didn't have much to lose.

———◆———

By the fall of 1987, we were starting to think about offering something besides dusters, in order to win new customers and get more orders from satisfied ones. I'd had in my mind a sort of pirate shirt for men, like the kind Errol Flynn dashed around in when he starred in *Captain Blood*. And then one day, reading a history magazine, I saw a picture of a simple Colonial American shirt with a full cut and big sleeves. The pirate shirt in my mind suddenly seemed too much like a costume. This one felt right. I remember thinking, "That's it. Wearing this would make me feel more like who I actually am." The thought had a familiar ring. I showed the picture to Don and Audrey and said, "Here's our next product, The J. Peterman Shirt." Audrey nodded approval. Don took a look and smiled. "Ah, yes. 99% Thomas Jefferson, 1% J. Peterman."

The shirt wasn't currently being made by someone else, as the duster still was at the time, so we couldn't just go out and buy it wholesale. I found a supplier who could provide us with good old-fashioned unbleached cotton muslin, bought the fabric, and took it to a sewing factory over in Pikeville, Kentucky. I had no concept of sizing at that point, or of anything else that went into making garments, but it worked. As orders began to come in, at a faster pace than we had anticipated, I began making twice-weekly trips to Pikeville to pick up shirts, about 120 miles round trip. Within two months, though, it became evident that the small outfit we were working with was not well run and couldn't keep up with the demand; our back orders were getting larger and larger. I found another factory in December. I remember shipping about 500 shirts out to customers three days before Christmas, paying the extra cost out-of-pocket for second-day air so that they would arrive in time for the holiday.

That knowledge of sourcing came in handy when our supplier of dusters began to behave erratically. Sometimes he would deliver on time, sometimes not. Eventually, he put us in a back-order bind as well. After I took that sample duster apart, I made call after call to find out where to buy snaps, where to buy nylon for the liner, corduroy for the collar, taping, and so forth. Then I found a manufacturer to put it all together. The process is called "cut, make, and sew." If you're a well-established company or have built up a relationship, manufacturers will source the components for you, but with "cut, make, and sew" they don't have to invest a nickel, and that's the way they all wanted it when they dealt with us.

Soon after The J. Peterman Shirt, we added The Alternative Duster to our product line—a hip-length version of the long original. Then came an authentic New York City Fireman's Coat, from the same company that makes them for real firemen, and a Baker Street Coat, modeled on the caped Inverness that Basil Rathbone wore when he played Sherlock Holmes. We sold them all as individual items through space ads. By early 1988, I could see that we had hit the limit with this one-item-at-a-time approach. As successful as the ads were, they weren't going to allow us to grow profitably. We needed a catalog to accompany each order we shipped, to advertise on its own, and to be mailed out to likely prospects whose names and addresses could be rented from list brokers.

So we started to plan for the first J. Peterman Owner's Manual, for the fall of 1988.

———◆———

Up until that point I had mostly financed the company myself, first with $500 out of pocket, then with an unsecured $20,000 loan from a local bank. In October of 1987, our first investors, my friends Cotton Nash and Lee Shultz, each kicked in $25,000. I also secured a $200,000 SBA-guaranteed loan at about that same time. At some point in early spring of 1988, I realized that the company would need a much bigger influx of capital. Inventory was taking up more and more money, as was advertising. I also had about seven people on the payroll, including Don, Audrey, our artist, Bob Hagel, and a few neighbors and friends who helped us take orders. And we were committed to doing the catalog. My banker had been blunt. "John," he said, "banks loan money, charge interest, and expect to be paid back. Loans are not capital. You need capital or you won't be able to get loans." I got the message. I didn't even know what a venture capitalist was, but I understood that I needed one badly.

When I think back on my first business plan now, I'm amazed at how rudimentary it was. The written credentials of the management team were thin, and we had no real substantiation of our market potential. I called 100 venture-capital firms, sent plans to 25 or 30, and got five or six face-to-face meetings. The script at the meetings was usually the same. They would look down at the business plan the way a teacher might look at a semi-literate term paper, then look up at me and say, "Tell us about your experience in the catalog business."

"I don't have any," I'd reply.

"Tell us about your experience in the apparel business."

"I don't have any."

"Well, in that case, you'll have to look for your money someplace else."

———————◆———————

We had some near misses with a few venture-capital firms before finally getting a hit. The real cliffhanger was the deal I almost struck with Smith & Hawken and Rockefeller & Company. I had sent out a business plan to the Rockefeller people, and they set up a meeting with a gent named Tom Barry and his young assistant, Jane Freeman. Tom was put together like a Princeton man; Jane seemed somewhat stiff, though she went to great lengths to be pleasant. I learned later that this was her first negotiation. I still didn't really know what I was doing, either, even though I had been turned down 96 times before. I was hopeful, excited, anxious.

The bloom was on the catalog business right then (a bloom that seems to come and go quickly), and they said something like, "We're intrigued with what you're doing. Whom do you respect in this business?" I mentioned Smith & Hawken, which struck a chord with them; one of the women in the Rockefeller family had spent time with Paul Hawken in a commune, and later invested in his company.

Tom and Jane didn't think I knew enough about catalog marketing to pull it off; they wanted someone more experienced to guide us. They said that if Smith & Hawken would invest in my company, then they would invest as well. The next day I was on a plane to California. I met Paul and toured his facilities. He turned out to be a fan of our advertising and appreciated what we were doing. Yes, he said, he'd be interested. He would be in New York in a few days, and we could meet with the Rockefeller people together.

I flew back East and the next night, very late, Paul phoned from an airplane en route to New York. He asked when I was scheduled to talk with the Rockefeller people next. "Tomorrow," I replied. "Don't make a deal with them," he said. "We've got money now." A vitamin manufacturer had just invested $23 million in his company, he explained. Everything seemed to click into place. Rockefeller had capital but no catalog expertise—and if Smith & Hawken could provide financing, I wouldn't need anyone else.

The following day I reluctantly kept my appointment with Rockefeller & Company. As we began to structure a deal involving puts and calls, which were rocket science to me, I kept thinking to myself, "I can't string this out. I can't negotiate in good faith here while I've got plans with Paul." So I told them I had to break off our conversation and told them why. I was honest, but naive.

Paul sent his chief financial officer to appraise our company's books—"due diligence," it's called. The books weren't up to Generally Accepted Accounting Principles but they were accurate to the best of our ability; the CFO seemed fine with them. Paul took the proposition to his board, and the next thing I knew he was yelling at me over the phone: "Those financials you gave me were garbage! They don't meet GAAP requirements!" I don't respond well to being yelled at. "Don't be a jerk, Paul!" I yelled back. "You sent your CFO in here, he saw the books, and you know damn well this is the best we've got. Don't say I've lied to you because I haven't."

Paul wasn't used to anybody talking to him like that. He calmed down very quickly. We kept negotiating through the fall of 1988, and in December I told him I was running out of money. He authorized a loan for $100,000. His board turned down the investment later that month, though. We found out on Christmas Eve.

I had to ask Paul to extend the loan, which he did, twice. Things got ugly in March of 1989—it looked as if Smith & Hawken was going to attempt some kind of hostile takeover because we couldn't pay them back. Fortunately, we got big backing in June; the debt was paid, and we all went on with our lives. I was angry with Paul for a while. I felt he had tried to take advantage. But the fact is, he loaned me the $100,000. He did the best he could. He hadn't realized that the $23 million invested in his company came with a board of directors attached, and he was no longer really in control.

———◆———

That whole period was hell, financially. Even with the $100,000 from Smith & Hawken, we ended up financing the company from January to June of 1989 on credit cards, $15,000 here, $15,000 there. Staley's. My own. I raised $65,000 that way to run more space ads, pay employees, and put out catalogs.

At one point we didn't have enough money to pay our vendors before a catalog came out. I called each one of them and promised I'd pay him $1,000 a week if he would just stick with us and continue to ship. They all did.

The catalogs were a huge success. That gave us revenue. It also created the need for even more expansion capital. So I decided to sell the cheese company. It wasn't hard to say goodbye; it had never made me much money, but the sale brought me a $250,000 return on my original $3,000 investment. Not bad. I decided to get out of consulting, too. That was a more difficult decision. I felt as if I were jettisoning my only safety net. Three of my four children were in college, two at the University of Kentucky at $6,500 each a year and one at Northwestern, at $18,000. Things would have been tight even without Dad's Duster Scheme. But I'd come to see that if The J. Peterman Company was going to work, I had to devote all my time to it. I also realized that I probably would never get anywhere with the venture capitalists if I continued to run other businesses. They don't like to invest in something if it isn't your full-time occupation.

The day after I'd made up my mind, the phone rang. A specialty-foods distributor in California needed a pricing study similar to one I'd done just the year before. They would pay $65,000. I stared out my window at a gravel truck loading up across the street. "I'm sorry," I said, "I'm no longer in the consulting business."

———◆———

June 1989. Finally. The call we'd been waiting for. It came from Hambro America, the venture capital arm of Hambro Bank of England. Edwin Goodman, who was its managing director at the time, had Alex Hambro, then a young man learning the family business, contact me. Alex identified himself, and asked if we were public. "No," I said. "We've seen your ads in the *New Yorker*," he continued, "and we're intrigued. Are you looking for capital?" I remember trying very hard to act nonchalant. "Possibly," I replied.

That was enough. Alex came down the next day for due diligence—it was a Thursday or Friday. Ed arrived Monday. We talked all day, then went to one of my favorite restaurants, Ramsay's, for an early dinner so he could catch a 7 P.M. flight back to New York. Over dinner, Ed asked me how much I thought the company was worth. I said three or four million. There's a lesson right there because he instantly latched onto the lower number. "Well, we'll invest $1.2 million," he said. We wrote the terms of the deal down on the proverbial napkin, which Ed took to his lawyers, and the legal papers came through in a week. I had a moment's panic when the papers at first didn't contain all of what Ed and I had talked about. I called him up, he looked the papers over. "You're right," he said, "we'll have this changed." And he did. We closed the deal in three weeks.

Ed, I believe, is the ultimate venture capitalist. He has his own firm now. He's smart. Decisive. He can be shrewd, but he's honest and his word is his bond. You'll find that venture capitalists often say one thing and when the legal paperwork comes back it's different from what was discussed, and then they'll deny that they said what they did originally. If I were a start-up company looking for seed capital, I'd go to Ed Goodman.

———◆———

At the time Hambro came along, our printer was threatening not to produce the next Owner's Manual unless I could somehow guarantee payment. Even though we hadn't closed the deal yet, Ed and Alex sent the printer a letter: "We're investing $1.2 million in The J. Peterman Company. Print the catalog. We're your guarantee."

That capital marked a turning point in the history of the company. It allowed us to grow from $1.2 million in sales in 1988 to $4.8 in 1989 and then $19.8 in 1990. Our staff went from 15 people in 1989 to about 75 or 80 in 1990. And my personal consumption of Maalox® declined.

We could also pay attention to practical matters like computer systems. We'd started out taking orders by hand, writing them into log books. If a customer returned something, you had to page through the log books, the way you did in the 1880s. A friend from the Jobe's days, Ron Elliott, created a basic order-entry system on our only PC in mid-1987. Next year we purchased a semi-antique System 34 IBM computer with three terminals and a printer; Ron designed a program for that as well. The Hambro money let us finally move up to a state-of-the-art AS400 with a complete fulfillment-system software package. We were a serious company now, with the iron to prove it.

———◆———

There were no exotic ports of call during those first three years. Most of the traveling I did was back and forth to New York, trying to get money, and back and forth to different manufacturers in Kentucky, trying to get products made. Even typical days weren't at all boring, though. We were creating something. I was passionate about what we were creating, even if I wasn't sure how it would turn out, and that passion helped to energize us all.

I usually started the day with breakfast at the Saratoga, a few blocks from our office. It was an old restaurant in an early 1900s building, dingy and dark, but it served good homemade food. It's gone now; I worry about places like that closing, the same way I worry that some day we're all going to wake up and find that there's no one alive who really knows how to build a good Rumford fireplace. Sometimes I'd see Bunker Hunt in there, with a consoling double order of sausage and pancakes. He was the son of Lamar Hunt, who owned the Dallas Cowboys and had made his fortune in the oil business.

Bunker was a "good ol' boy" who wore size XXX khakis and denim shirts. At one time he had the most horse-farm land and the most racehorses in Kentucky. Then he tried to corner the silver market, drove the price of silver from about $5 an ounce to about $40 before everything collapsed and they took all his horses and land away. There was a lesson there, too.

I'd get to the office at about 8 A.M. to work on finding manufacturers, solve inventory problems . . . the box maker hadn't delivered, what was the holdup? A myriad of operational details. And I'd talk to Don on the phone every day, for two or three hours. We'd discuss copy, ideas, products, places, experiments. It used to drive other people in the office crazy because it didn't look like work, but Don and I never communicated in a way that was even remotely corporate. He once sent me a memo that went like this:

> To: John Peterman—
>
> Since I will be spending the entire day in New York City going from bar to bar, riding around in limousines, going to art exhibits, ordering suits, browsing through piles of cashmeres, talking to Soviet attachés, it will be up to you therefore, to solve these mundane problems:
>
> N. Yorker (1/9) closing 12/21 (Wed.)—all the type shops here will be closed, drinking champagne, swallowing smoked oysters & caviar mixed together—how about mailbag and duster (No. 1 and No. 3 $ items)?

*Then GQ for Mar. (you said maybe skip), the 3
coats (fire/Bk. St./duster)?*

*Then NYT Mag. (1/22) navy grip+mbg (yes, two
bags).*

Gradually, Don and I developed a full lineup of wonderful products. Some came from my experience, like The J. Peterman Shirt, or a men's one-piece black bathing suit with shoulder straps, a powerful looking thing I'd seen in an old photograph of my dad as a young man at the beach. Don tended to contribute upscale stuff, like the Swaine Adeney Brigg umbrella, a magnificent apparatus built like a pre-WWII Bentley and favored by the Queen of England. The best products often reflected an overlap of our interests, like a men's wallet made out of baseball-mitt leather:

Stop and think about that wonderful dark pocket of leather in the middle of a baseball glove, lovingly used and punished for half a lifetime. Is it wearing out? Is it ready to throw away? No, it's just quietly getting better.

Our first two catalogs did better than we'd dared to hope, but the illustrations were all black and white and they were short on product—the initial one had five items—"miserable little things," Don called them. The third catalog, for spring and summer of 1989, set the pattern for those that followed. It offered an unpredictable mix of stuff, 21 items in all, from Babe Ruth's baseball bat to a terrycloth robe with the logo of the old Shepheard's Hotel in Cairo, Egypt, each respectfully assigned its own page and illustrated in color, each meeting the criteria Don and I had in mind: well-made, unique or hard-to-find, with factual romance to it, an authenticity linked to a time or place your imagination could enjoy traveling to.

We held an impromptu party in my office the afternoon the first cartons of Owner's Manual No. 3 arrived from the printer. Brought up a case of Fall City beer from the cheese-making room, ceremoniously opened a carton of catalogs, and handed them out for inspection. Much excitement, mutual congratulations . . . then I noticed Audrey's dad by the pot-bellied stove, studying his copy with a slight frown. I walked over to him. "What do you think?" I asked.

He took a reflective sip of Fall City. "This doesn't look like any catalog I ever saw," he said. "It looks like some kind of . . . *art.*"

The Golden Rule is that there are no golden rules.

—G. B. Shaw (1856–1950)

"Peterman, You Must Be Crazy"

The direct-marketing expert was tapping his pen on the table, already mentally on board the flight to his next meeting up in Cleveland. He looked at me in a sort of pitying way. "Your catalog hasn't got a chance, John. There are rules to this business, you know. You've managed to break just about every one of them."

Guilty as charged.

The Owner's Manual had an odd, oblong shape, 5-1/2" × 10-1/2", and wasn't even identified as a catalog. "Consumers won't understand what an 'Owner's Manual' is, and they're not sitting around waiting to solve puzzles." Our use of artwork to show products raised eyebrows. "Consumers don't trust drawings, they want to see photographs of what they're buying." Long copy instead of short, to-the-point product descriptions was risky. "Consumers don't have time to read; besides, their attention spans are short, anyway."

And selling one item per page was suicidal to the "square-inchers"—the guys who try to calculate profit per square inch of catalog space. "You need 2.7 items on a page if you want to make any money."

Now, there may be an element of truth to all that if you're selling familiar, standardized stuff. But we were offering uncommon things to people who had to be willing to be different—people like ourselves. So we took a deep breath and went with an approach that appealed to us.

———◆———

My dad wasn't an eccentric character. He didn't read Henry Miller and Jack Kerouac. He seemed conservative on the surface, working for the same employer for 48 years, going from mail clerk to loan officer at the Irving Trust Company. In his own quiet way, though, he was a contrarian. Back in 1938, before I was born, he moved the family out of New York City, where he and my mother had both been raised, to an agrarian community in Rockland County. A group of people had purchased an old Dutch farm and divided it into small parcels ranging from one to five acres. Everyone who bought into the community agreed to build their own house and grow a substantial part of their own food.

My dad's choice of this alternative way of life made a strong impression on me. It said that it was OK to march to a different drummer.

We did a lot of work together on the house, which wasn't completely finished until I was twelve or thirteen. I helped him lay flooring upstairs, dig out a back room in the basement, install a septic system. We worked the land together, too. I learned how to grow vegetables, prune fruit trees, and other skills that may come in handy again if the survivalists prove to be right.

We didn't talk much. I learned more by osmosis than by lectures. But I do recall a few conversations, including one when I was about seven. I'd been playing cowboys and Indians with the neighbors' kids and as usual, for some reason, I'd chosen to be an Indian. My dad took me aside and told me that I was in fact one-sixteenth part Iroquois. That knowledge became a magic talisman. It meant that being different from my friends and other people I knew was built into me.

Later, another family member made an impression, too. Uncle Joe was my mother's brother. He used to show up in limousines, tall, handsome, flamboyant, equipped with a hip flask and big rolls of $20 and $50 bills—totally out of place in Rockland County. Uncle Joe was a Marine during WWII; he was there on Iwo Jima when they raised that flag. After the war he became a newspaperman in the hard-drinking *Front-Page* tradition. He saw through the polite smiles and hat tipping of everday life into the dark heart of man and found it full of hidden agendas. He knew What Really Went On in the world of politics.

I used to go to the races with Uncle Joe. One time at the betting window he gave me five dollars. "John," he said, "put this on Thunderbolt to place in the fourth."

"Uncle Joe, Thunderbolt is the worst horse on the track."

"John, put the five dollars on Thunderbolt."

I reluctantly obeyed and was then astonished when several horses collided near the finish line, miraculously allowing Thunderbolt to come in second. Suddenly I was holding more cash than I'd ever had before at one time. "How did you know to bet on Thunderbolt?" I asked.

Uncle Joe reached out, clasped my shoulder, and gave me a somber look:

"John, the races are fixed."

———◆———

Once you realize that most people are keeping up appearances and putting on a show, their approval becomes much less important.

———◆———

To me, then, at any rate, the phrase "Owner's Manual" made sense. It sounded valuable, like something you'd find in the glove compartment of your Duesenberg. I liked the odd catalog shape because it stood out from the typical clutter in the mailbox; for a while there, we also got a discount from the post office by using that size. Bob Hagel's illustrations were far more expressive to me than any photography a catalog could afford. And I knew that I, for one, was willing to read long copy as long as it was interesting:

> *The morning was going to be special.*
>
> *Privacy. Absolutely no phones.*
>
> *She read him his horoscope, translating the German. She sliced him a peach, peeling it into one continuous helix, like a maître d' in a restaurant.*
>
> *But quite unlike any maître d' either of them had ever seen, she now proceeded to slide each slice slowly between his lips, through his teeth, into his waiting mouth.*
>
> *All this, and the rest of it, went fairly smoothly until he broke out laughing, and went to sleep. She watched his chest for a while.*

They both remembered the mood long, long
afterwards.
Certain details too.
She remembered his horoscope.
He remembered the peaches. And her.

Experts might not see the connection between such writing and the item it eventually got around to selling—a silk "October Weekend Skirt" borrowed from a 1930s English garden party—but my bet was that women would have no problem at all. They'd feel it. And if they did, we'd sell a lot more skirts off the page than a "square-incher" would predict.

———◆———

If people wanted to boost their nerve quotient a bit, to feel more comfortable about taking chances in pursuit of a worthwhile aim, I might suggest that they get involved in some kind of competitive sport.

You're playing tennis, for example, and the ball streaks across the net toward the edge of the court. If you really want to win the game, you'll stretch yourself to deliver the return—maybe make a dash and throw yourself sideways in what would ordinarily seem a foolhardy maneuver. When you succeed, even if you scrape your elbow or skin your knee, you'll feel exhilarated at having done something outside the norm.

You'll feel the stretch was worth it, even as you walk off in search of Bacitracin®. You'll be more likely to take a risk next time, because of the reward you just won. And you'll be that much more likely to take similar steps off the court, in the rest of your life.

That's the way sports have worked for me, anyway. I learned early on that taking risks paid off. The praise I got was sweet. And the confidence I gained didn't stay confined to the ballfield, but carries me to this day.

I recall one game, in particular, at Holy Cross. It was at the original Fitton Field, which was in its glory during the 1940s and early 1950s, when the Red Sox would come to play the Holy Cross team; I have an autographed picture of Ted Williams at bat there, sent to me by a customer who had learned that Holy Cross was my alma mater.

The stands at Fitton were old and creaky by my time, and my coach, "Hop" Riopel, seemed kind of old, too. Hop was from the Class of 1924, probably the best athlete ever to wear HC colors. He commanded respect, sometimes terror, from anyone he came into contact with. We never could figure out how he managed to smoke his cigarette in the shower without getting it wet. He ruled us firmly—I can still recite the infield-fly rule verbatim because of him—and in his warmest moments, he radiated crust.

It was early spring, us against Dartmouth, with me playing third. The air was chilly; we were grateful for our itchy wool

71

uniforms. One of the Dartmouth guys drove a base hit into right field and the 200-pounder on first saw his chance to round second and get to third. As he charged in my direction, the right fielder grabbed the ball on the bounce and made a perfect throw to me. I just stood there, not letting on that the throw was coming, so the big guy didn't realize the threat and kept running instead of going into a slide. Then, suddenly, I had the ball, the big guy was right on top of me, I tagged him head on, and spun out of his path. I could have stepped to the side and tried to tag him as he went by, but this was the only way to guarantee the out. I sprained my wrist; the astonishment on the runner's face, the out, and what Hop said to me after made it worthwhile, though. When we went in to bat, he walked over to me and looked me straight in the eye. "That was a hell of a play," he said. "You're the kind of player I want."

I'd never gotten a compliment from him before, and I never got one again, not even when I batted .450 in the College Series. Just that one time, when I risked my neck to win.

◆

The Jesuit-founded College of the Holy Cross in Worcester, Massachusetts, was in many respects a bastion of conformity. You had to wear a tie and jacket to all classes, and stand up respectfully when instructors entered the classrooms. Ten-thirty P.M. curfew was strictly enforced by the priests, who monitored each floor of the dormitories. Every evening, you sat at the same table in the 2,000-place dining room. You said grace first, then dug into the wholesome but monotonous food—a perpetual cycle of pot roast, spaghetti, ham, chicken, pork chops, and fish on Fridays. I remember lots of potatoes, and some very gluey scallops.

You had to attend Mass each day, too; the challenge there was to stay awake. It was easy to doze off as you knelt in the hot chapel with your forehead on the pew in front of you. Priests roamed the aisles, reprimanding anyone who nodded off, and frequent offenders were sent to the Dean's office, a dark, intimidating little cell with a small window and one dimly lit lamp. We would appoint someone in our row to be the Watcher, and when a priest got close, the Watcher would nudge the fellow next to him, who would nudge the next fellow, and so on. The system worked reasonably well; still, I saw the inside of the Dean's office more than I would have liked.

Holy Cross was a men's college in my day, mostly Irish Catholic, with a few Italians; I envy the diversity they have on campus now. The main expansion of my social horizon was to hobnob with my upper-middle-class schoolmates. I used to go down to Boston with Charlie O'Connor, whose dad was a well-connected contractor; the O'Connor home was easily three times the size of our place in Rockland County, solid stone, with starched lace curtains that had been stretched and dried in oak frames to a cardboard-like stiffness.

On Sunday afternoons I'd join the family at their big dining table for a meal of roast beef served by the house-keeper, Bridie. Conversation would often turn in a familiar way to "Jack" and "Bobby" and "Teddy" and the late James Michael Curley, four-time mayor of Boston. Yes, he'd been a rascal, he should never have used Massachusetts State Troop-ers as golf caddies, but you had to admit that the man had built a marvelous number of much-needed hospitals, schools, and roads.

For all its sameness, Holy Cross could be liberal about intellectual matters; well, open, anyway. Although Galileo was still condemned by the Church at that point, the good Jesuit fathers had no problem with explaining how he had set up the basis of modern science—you make a hypothesis, design an experiment to test it, and then see if the results bear you out. For 1,800 years, everybody had blindly accepted Aristotle's common-sense view that heavy things fall faster than light ones. Then Galileo dropped two different weights off the Leaning Tower of Pisa at the same time and found, as he'd expected, that the heavy one and the light one hit the ground simultaneously. Good-bye, Aristotle.

I liked that.

Part of our training also came straight from classic rhet-oric, which taught that there were at least two sides to every story; an educated person should be able to argue contradictory points of view thoughtfully. I recall Father O'Hara, our history professor, peering over his gold-rimmed glasses and posing an unexpected question:

"Gentlemen, how many of you believe in the existence of God?"

All hands shot up reflexively.

"Well, can you offer any evidence of His Being?"

A much smaller, hesitant response. "Father," replied a brave soul, "the Church and all Her teachings are predicated on God."

" 'Predicated.' Very good. But consider these facts. The American Civil War, with 600,000 casualties. Twenty million casualties in World War I. Fifty million in World War II. The bombing of Dresden and Hiroshima, the atrocities of the Holocaust. Gentlemen, how can you possibly reconcile such terrible events with the existence of a just and merciful Creator?"

We sat dumbfounded as Father O'Hara paused to polish his glasses, then continued with a thin smile:

"Now, on the *other* hand . . ."

———◆———

Subscribe to the *Economist* and the *Utne Reader* as well as *Time* and *Newsweek*. Try Ethiopian food. Strike up a conversation with a truck driver. It's a big world.

Sometimes you scrape your elbow, and you don't win the match; you have to expect that. What's harder to swallow is when you prove to be right about something and people simply won't acknowledge it. That's what happened to Galileo—his findings outraged true believers so much that the Inquisition put him under house arrest and told him to keep quiet.

I ran into that same side of human nature on a modest scale when I was sales and marketing manager for Jobe's Fertilizer Spikes. The owner of the company had a fine little patented product; just push the spikes into the soil and you nourish your plants and trees at the roots, for months, with no risk of over feeding. During my three years with Jobe's, sales grew from $700,000 to $21 million, thanks to a simple strategy. We made a commercial and ran it just enough to create a buzz in the plant business, then told stores that this was the beginning of a national advertising campaign that would have consumers breaking down the doors. We got eye-catching product displays in all sorts of stores that way, and because the spikes were an impulse purchase, we did in fact sell truckloads of them.

I spent a lot of time in the field, talking with customers. Eventually, I learned that Kmart, our biggest customer, was interested in us doing a private-label version of the product for them. The owner wouldn't hear of it, though, and he thought that no one could get around his patent. Well, Kmart went ahead and created its own brand anyway, and I think the man went into what is technically called "denial." When I learned soon after that Pathmark and Safeway wanted private labels, too, I pitched him as strongly as I could not to let the same thing happen again. "I'm sorry to let you go, John," he said, "but you're not sticking with the program."

The next year, I was in the consulting business, the other chains had their own brands, and Jobe's sales fell to $11 million.

———◆———

The unconventional format of our catalog wasn't all that offended the experts, of course; they thought the merchandise we were selling was too offbeat to gain much of an audience. "There aren't enough kooky college professors out there to buy your stuff," a venture capitalist once told me.

What really troubled the fellow was that here were things that didn't happen to appeal to him, personally, and we couldn't point to a mountain of market research that "proved" they'd be welcomed by anybody else, either.

Ordinarily, companies do extensive testing of products before they screw up the courage to put them into stores. They're very fond of focus groups, where consumers led by a moderator give their reactions to new-product concepts while researchers and ad-agency people watch from behind a one-way mirror.

The process can be helpful if you frame questions right and look at the results in an enlightened way, without taking them as dictation. Often, though, it elicits enough negative opinions for fearful managers to smother good ideas in the cradle. It encourages compromises that appeal to the lowest common denominator, or leads to disasters like the Edsel and New Coke®. And it tends to drag on. I know of a company that spent two years testing bottle designs for a new brand of spring water—by which time the competition had divvied up the market.

The beauty of direct marketing is that you can test products (or creative approaches or media choices or whatever) much faster, and have more faith in the results. Within a few weeks of mailing a catalog, you know if a certain item is a winner or a dog based on actual, real-world sales, as opposed to people in a focus group saying, "Yes, I'd buy that" or "Not in a million years, I *hate* pink." It's the Galileo method, and it pays to use it boldly.

That's what we did with the Owner's Manual and our second catalog, Booty, Spoils & Plunder, introduced in the early 1990s to offer hard goods and collectibles. We opened up product areas that hardly existed before. And we sold more than a few items that I must admit struck me as peculiar, but then, you never know unless you try.

Early on, while poking around the dusty offices of a shirtmaker who was working for us, we came upon the original patterns for a collarless men's shirt from the 1920s. Having a collar *sewn* onto your shirt in those days was unthinkable; you removed your detachable collar whenever it got slightly soiled or went limp (this was before air conditioning) and attached a spotless, crisp, fresh one by means of a button on the back of the collar band.

The shirt struck me as a more refined version of our J. Peterman Shirt, so we had some made up and put it in the catalog. Don christened it The Gatsby Shirt, with a nod to those shirts in *The Great Gatsby* that were so beautiful, they made Daisy Buchanan weep:

> *The cotton we have used in our uncompromising replica of Gatsby's shirt is so luminous, in and of itself, that even a person who notices nothing will notice something. Gatsby, of course, could afford stacks of these shirts; rooms of them. Never mind. All that matters is that you have one, just one. A piece of how things were.*

The collarless Gatsby Shirt was an instant success. Hmm, we thought, what else did people wear back then that might have appeal today? Soon, we were selling cloche hats, tennis dresses from around 1912 ("the last summer before income tax"), ankle-length suffragette skirts with long rows of buttons. When Ralph Lauren's Polo began to draw inspiration from our items—I saw at least one check to us with the Polo name on it—I knew that we had started a trend to period clothing.

As the owner of a 1935 Auburn Boattail Speedster (designed by Gordon Buehrig of Duesenberg fame), I was fascinated by another item, a vintage BMW R71 motorcycle with a one-passenger sidecar. It wasn't actually made by BMW; the R71 tooling and designs had fallen into Soviet hands at the end of WWII and were passed on to the Chinese, who produced the bike for the People's Liberation Army until 1967. The Chinese had a warehouse full of them, all surplus, still in their original crates.

I bought one and took some of our merchants for a test ride. Top speed was only 53 mph, but it had a wonderful back-road, baguette, bottle-of-wine, and thou quality. How much would we charge? "$7,500," I replied. "John, you're crazy," said one of the merchants; the price was too high for a catalog. Nevertheless, we sold $560,000 worth of gloriously obsolete machinery.

Maybe the quirkiest thing we ever offered was a gold-plated English monocle on a long silk cord, available in three magnifying strengths. I didn't know exactly what to make of it, but it certainly was unique and hard to find. We went ahead and announced "The Return of the Monocle," with a sketch of the device and some disarming copy:

"Good grief, Peterman, do you want me to look like Erich von Stroheim?"

Relax, I'm not suggesting that at all.

It's just that a monocle is more convenient and less ostentatious than carrying around a magnifying glass for tasks eyeglasses aren't up to, like examining NASDAQ listings or the wings of a Vanessa atalanta.

Later, for private amusement, you might practice holding it in your eye, just as Napoleon, Beethoven, and other famous monocle-wearers have done before you. There's an art to this. Please note extensions on the top and bottom of the frame ("galleries") designed to help it stay put.

There you have it. Perfectly sensible, plus an option for hours, months, a lifetime, of drollery.

We also included a whimsical sidebar—a small box filled with tiny type, entitled "Monocle Method":

Ca. 1806. The monocle as we now know it originates on the English stage. Standardized monocle gestures soon develop to signify emotions with no facial expressions required, e.g., slowly removing monocle indicates anger; letting monocle drop from eye and bounce on waistcoat indicates surprise; inserting monocle indicates one is about to launch a shaft of wit.

Somewhat to my own surprise, we received 5,000 orders at $90 each; we had tapped into a pent-up demand for monocles. As our "Philosophy" statement on the inside front cover of every Owner's Manual put it, "Clearly, people want things that make their lives the way they wish they were."

If one advances confidently in the
direction of his dreams, he will meet with
a success unexpected in common hours.

—H. D. Thoreau (1817–1862)

The Catalog That
Started a Cult

"Two eggs over easy, crisp bacon, hold the grits." Sarah, my usual waitress at the Saratoga, knew my breakfast order by heart. This morning, though, in November 1990, she brought something extra on the tray: a newspaper with an article circled.

"Special of the day, John," she said.

I took a closer look. It was a piece by Tom Peters, the best-known business thinker of our time, writing on a subject close to me:

> I wish the J. Peterman Co. of Lexington, Ky., would win the 1991 Malcolm Baldrige National Quality Award. Their Winter 1990 catalog, "Owner's Manual No. 8," just arrived; as usual, I dropped what I was doing and sat down to read it.

No photos, just hand-drawn illustrations. And wonderful, whimsical text. . . . The J. Peterman catalog is fun. The products and presentation are "world-class quality" writ large. A few thousand more J. Petermans and we could kiss our economic woes goodbye.

I didn't need sugar in my coffee after that.

A fairly steady rain of other articles soon began to appear, like one by Holly Brubach, in *The New York Times Sunday Magazine*, that made me check my hat size:

The stuff of J. Peterman's catalogue copy—the acute powers of observation, the delight in the smallest details of everyday life and the urge to record them—is the stuff of literature and it sets J. Peterman apart from his fellow mail-order entrepreneurs: he is a merchant poet.

The fact is, I never had myself confused with the charming fellow that people sensed was there, just out of reach, behind the words on our catalog pages; he was the product of more than one mind. But my memories and convictions went into him. I was delighted, once, to come across a certain small detail of life from long ago—a pair of fawn-colored leather spats. I had no intention of reproducing the spats for sale; instead, we ran a drawing of them with copy entitled "Circa 1906," to express something of what I felt the company stood for:

They are old. They are useless. But they are beautiful.

I bought them at a vintage clothing sale—not to sell, but as a reminder of how well stuff used to be made: pearl buttons 1/8" thick, leather seams with 14 stitches per inch.

They also remind me of more recent things, which (amazingly) we've given up with hardly a murmur of protest.

Peaches worth eating and doctors who make house-calls. Real starch in shirt collars. Bakelite. Books sewn in signatures. Strike-anywhere matches. Soapbox orators. Car engines you can tune yourself. Meaningful S.A.T. scores. Lüchow's, foghorns, taffeta dresses, and sparklers on July 4th.

Isn't it time to take some kind of stand here?

I'm saving all I can. I hope you are too.

I guess that is as close to poetry as you'll find in a mail-order catalog.

———◆———

A recent friend of mine told me that years ago, late at night on Nantucket, she and her housemates used to sit in their water-front rental, listening to the waves break on Tom Nevers beach, drinking Barolo, and reading from the Owner's Manual. "Steff was getting married that summer," she said. "I needed a dress to wear to the wedding, and she needed something to wear to a cocktail party in her honor. We started reading our catalogs out loud as we were looking through them, and soon, the others were in on the act. We'd start with the copy that was there, then make up our own finishes. Or we'd 'introduce' one product to another—'The tall, thin, brooding man in the J. Peterman Shirt meets the woman wearing the Flip-Up Sunglasses at Café de Flore, 1 A.M. sharp; secret documents are exchanged.'

"Knowing about the catalog was sort of an inside thing," she said. "It was like being a member of a club, and you felt more a part of it with each issue."

People loved to read the Owner's Manual even if they never actually bought anything. When we'd take them off the mailing list, eventually, they'd write letters pleading with us to put them back on again. Some customers confided that they bought an item once a year or so to make sure that they didn't miss a mailing. Fortunately, others bought a lot more.

(As the catalogs kept coming out, getting thicker and thicker, direct-marketing experts became converts, too; they called us "the anti-catalog," and meant it as a compliment.)

Many people related to the catalog in a very personal way, almost as if it were a letter written by a good friend who can take you out of yourself, out of your routine—or remind you of who you really are. We told stories, gave candid opinions and confidential advice. We often spoke in an intimate one-on-one way, as in this copy for our Women's Tuxedo Shirt:

The question, really, is how did you get by this long without it? No wonder you've been a little sulky; I know I'm not the only one who's noticed it.

In return, readers weren't shy about letting us know when we pleased or displeased them. We once took a matching tweed jacket and pants that had a wonderful, gentleman-in-the-country quality and named them the "E. Digby Baltzell Memorial Tweeds," in tribute to the dapper sociologist who wrote *The Protestant Establishment* and invented the acronym "WASP":

"You must meet the WASP man," hostesses would say. A dashing figure at the Germantown Cricket Club, around the quad at Penn. Invariably wore candy-striped shirts and bow ties with his tweeds, although he'd defend, in principle, your right to do otherwise.

A former student wrote in, outraged: how dare we exploit the great man for our tawdry commercial purposes? But Mrs. Baltzell wrote to us, too. She thoroughly enjoyed the copy. The suit was just like the ones her late husband favored.

There was going to be a symposium in his honor, and all his old colleagues would be wearing the Memorial Tweeds.

The Owner's Manual was filled with references to Alexander the Great, the Russian Navy, Kanchanaburi, Tolstoi and Vita Sackville-West, Ludwig Wittgenstein and chaos theory, Georgia O'Keeffe, "Bear" Bryant, Gable and Harlow, and Wendy Hiller, some of them pretty obscure. "Thanks for bringing back memories of my rum-running days," someone would tell us. Or, "Where can I get that P. D. Ouspensky book you referred to?" When we made errors, occasionally, vigilant readers were quick to respond. "Churchill was elected in April but he didn't move to 10 Downing until *October.*" "You can't 'clubhaul a ketch.'"

Several times, scrupulous college professors wrote in for an OK to use our material in their literature classes. Well, why not? We offered everything from fresh aphorisms ("A shirt is the pedestal upon which a human face stands to present its case") to whole novels condensed into a few paragraphs, like this copy for our WWII Canadian Air Force Duffelbag:

> *A farmer's son, growing up in Alberta, Canada, sees a lot of sky.*
>
> *It sets him dreaming.*
>
> *At 16 he's flying a crop duster.*
>
> *At 23 he's an RCAF volunteer in the Battle of Britain. Bader's 242 Squadron. A Hawker Hurricane of his own.*

Scrambling twice a day to intercept German ME 109s soon convinces him that he is not, in fact, immortal. But there are compensations.

At the pub in Duxford, the wings on his uniform have a persuasive effect on the local solicitor's daughter.

(Other envious soldiers are now referring to fighter pilots as "The Brylcreem Boys.")

No question of marriage. Not until he's demobbed. And that will happen in '43, thanks to fragments of a 7.92mm slug encountered over France.

He will limp a bit walking down the aisle.

She will think he never looked more handsome.

It wasn't only the writing that was admired. Collectors asked (and still do) to buy Bob Hagel's artwork. People who know about these things say Hagel has a line that can't be confused with that of any other artist; it gets to the essence of things in an energetic, unhesitating way that's never merely pretty to look at.

Some customers even wanted to collect *me*. I received quite a few mash notes from ladies all over the world inviting me to dinner, if ever I were in their neighborhood. One California woman applied for a position with the company as a massage therapist; she enclosed a nude photo of herself leaning against a fine specimen of an elm tree.

Little did she know that Audrey, my wife, was in charge of the mailroom, and opened all my mail before I got it.

———◆———

The rapport that customers had with the company showed in another remarkable way: they often turned to us as a kind of Society for Historic Preservation, sending in things they were afraid might disappear from the face of the Earth unless we reproduced them—an authentic old Norfolk jacket, a 1928 Air Corps briefcase, a great-great grandmother's blouse.

Our earliest "customer-sourced" item was The Counterfeit Mailbag. A retired mailman from Houston sent us the mailbag that had served him for 30 years, thick leather with a large rounded flap in front, a style discontinued by the cost accountants. Some details were missing, so I got another from a former letter carrier in Lexington and found a manufacturer; the bag went on to become as much a perennial as the J. Peterman Shirt:

> *The secret thoughts of an entire nation were carried in leather bags exactly like this one. . . . I borrowed an original from a friend, a retired mailman who, like thousands before him, was kind enough to test it out, for years, on the tree-lined streets of small towns everywhere. Before you were born.*

A few years later, we had a surge in consignments of WWII military uniforms and equipment, like Army shirts with buttoning neck flaps to protect against possible mustard-gas attacks; we put together a collection and ran a piece entitled "We Were Soldiers Once, and Young":

I think the 50th Anniversary of D-Day sparked it.

Veterans around the country got up from the 6:30 news to rummage through closets and battered trunks, emerging with wonderful WWII gear, a lot of which they forwarded to us: "Can you do something with this?"

Here are three of the items. Faithful reproductions of shirts in which they trained, fought, grumbled, flirted with Red Cross doughnut girls, and when you come down to it, saved the world.

That one didn't produce any big sellers, but I felt I owed it to Uncle Joe.

———◆———

The J. Peterman Company was looking good from the outside during the early 1990s, and it looked good to us on the inside, too. Revenues grew from $19.8 million in 1990 to $45 million 1992. Profitability was up. We moved to bigger offices in an industrial park on Palumbo Drive. They were palatial compared with Midland Avenue; there was even a tree in front.

It felt like the sky was the limit.

We had done a lot of in-house training up until that point—my assistant Paula Collins, for example, developed into one of the best merchants in the business. I kept that policy, but I also realized that we had to have seasoned, professional help with our increasingly complex finances and our growing need for new products. In April 1990 I hired John Rice as our CFO and head of operations, and in October I brought Tom Holzfeind on board as our first vice president of merchandising.

John was at Haband, the mail-order giant run by Duke Habernickel, "The Prince of Polyester," which sells a million pairs of pants a month. He hadn't been looking for a job. I won him over because we were a more exciting place to be, and, on a pragmatic level, we were offering options. He had always wanted to work someplace where he could be more than just an employee, he told me. John hit the ground running, spending his first two weeks at Commercialware, our software provider in Boston, nailing down our new fulfillment system. We were soon taking orders, shipping product, and getting paid like clockwork.

Tom came from the ritzier Horchow catalog operation, where he worked directly with the legendary Roger Horchow as head of merchandising; he now runs the Smithsonian Catalogue. Tom grasped the Peterman concept right away. His taste was impeccable. He knew what it takes to put a catalog together. He'd developed good agent contacts on his travels overseas. And he was secure in himself, with none of the confrontational attitude that is all too common in the world of retail, merchandising, and catalogs. That made him an excellent teacher who played a major role in developing our merchants.

On the creative side of the business, Don seemed reluctant to share responsibility for writing the catalog—he could create a perfect world there, where he had absolute control—but he was having a tough time turning out dozens of new pieces for each edition by himself. He tried a number of big-name copywriters, without much success, before enlisting Bill McCullam, who became the senior writer for the company until we closed our doors. Bill had been a creative director on BMW and Waterford Crystal, among other upscale advertising accounts, and had started in direct marketing; some of his direct-response print ads and TV commercials had run profitably for over ten years. Later, he was joined by a select group of other writers including Amy Bloom, author of the novel *Love Invents Us* and a National Book Award finalist.

———◆———

One day in 1992, I realized as I was walking through the halls that I didn't recognize all my employees anymore. I was hiring managers and interviewing prospective merchants, but there were a lot more souls coming on board than that—John Rice was hiring, Audrey (reporting to John) was bringing in customer-service reps, the warehouse manager was staffing up, etc.

I didn't like not knowing the people who were working for me, and, more important, I didn't like them not having a firsthand sense of who I was. So I started to hold regular Friday breakfasts, a practice that lasted until 1997. My assistant would pick eight employees from around the company at random, all levels, all departments. We'd meet in my office and sit around my old Philippine mahogany poker table for a get-acquainted meal and conversation. This was not a bagels-and-orange-juice buffet. Waiters served scrambled eggs and Potatoes O'Brien and fresh fruit on real china. We used a House-of-Commons coffeepot and silverware. I'd ask questions to get to know everyone, and they'd ask questions, too—hesitantly, at first, but as the event became an established fixture, more freely. We'd cover any topic, from kids and restaurants to what we were selling, how the business was doing, what their ambitions were. We eventually held lunches, as well, because having to show up at 7:30 A.M. could put a strain on commuters.

Morale was excellent in the early 1990s. Turnover was very low. We were goal-oriented, not method-bound. People had freedom to solve problems the way they thought best. They could work their way up to responsible positions at a much earlier age than elsewhere, and legitimately feel identified with the company's success. There were lots of celebrations, too, brought off with skill by Audrey—company picnics, Christmas dances, Hallowe'en costume parties. I've heard rumors of a photograph showing me in a Roman toga, with a tilted laurel wreath on my head, standing next to John Rice decked out as Dame Edna, but no blackmail demands have been made yet.

One other thing: we trusted each other. Employees were often surprised at that, having come from companies where regimentation was the rule. I recall Robert Bolson, who'd been a dispatcher at the Lexington Police Department. He started as our head nighttime service rep when we were still on Midland Avenue and stayed with us until the end, ultimately becoming a writer. When Audrey gave him the keys to lock up on his first night, he looked at her in astonishment and smiled. "I'm going to like it here," he said.

———◆———

The catalog seemed to have an insatiable appetite for new products now. Tom, Paula, Don, and I were frequenting antique shows, small clothing shops from SoHo to Ghiardelli Square, and beginning to travel to Europe. We only wanted things that were unique or hard to find elsewhere.

We were way ahead of the curve on many items, and I'd say we launched the curve in some cases, like the collarless shirt and other period clothing. During Operation Desert Storm, we were the only place where civilians could obtain the same high-tech sunglasses issued to Stealth-bomber pilots in the Persian Gulf. We were also the first catalog to carry those chunky, comfortable walking shoes made by a certain French company called Mephisto. We bought our Mephistos from the person in charge of their U.S. distribution; it was one of the few times we purchased from a sales rep—they usually want to sell to as many outlets as they can, which guarantees the item won't be special—but the Mephisto man was just starting to figure out the territory, and his product really was wonderful:

Weeding my way through the jungle of "biomechanically perfect" and "orthopedically engineered" and "air-injected" running-jumping-springing-catapulting shoes out there, I believe I have found the ultimate walking shoe. (Walking, after all, is what most of us do most of the time.)

I met Martin Micheali, the owner of Mephisto, on my first European buying trip. Don and I took the train from Paris to Sarrebourg, where the Mephisto factory is. The Sarrebourg station has a large cobblestone square in front, and cars have to park on the other side. Only one car was there, with a gent I assumed to be Martin standing next to it. As we walked across the cobblestones to join him, he seemed to be appraising my gait. He held out his hand; "Peterman?" "Yes," I replied. "Hmm, I thought you'd be taller."

On the London leg of that first trip we stayed at Blakes Hotel, which became my standard for hotels and for customer service in general. Blakes is a small place in South Kensington, set in a row of 19th-century townhouses, and identified by a discreet brass wall plaque; it's favored by film and music types who value their privacy. I went up the front steps, through the large doors, across an intimate lobby that glowed like an Old Master painting (mirrors, dark burnished leather, mellow wood, baskets of oranges). "Ah, Mr. Peterman, we've been expecting you; you're checked in." No questions, no forms to fill out; I presented my credit card at the reception desk and that was it. From then on the entire staff did every-thing they could to make us feel like personal guests.

We spent a week "working" London, from Savile Row to Portobello Road to Jermyn Street, discovering hunting coats and Victorian carpet bags and a glorious bone-handled badger shaving brush which we sold with copy that captured the feeling of our expeditions:

Jermyn St., and nearby Old Bond St., are exactly what you (if you were an Englishman) might dream about, if you unexpectedly found yourself pinned beneath an avalanche of boulders at the bottom of the Min Gorge in China.

Waiting to be rescued, your mind might turn to the cool hushed perfection of all the tiny elegant shops along certain London streets, shops where clerks read your mind, anticipate your wishes, bringing forth soothing potions, perfectly fitted shoes, impeccable linen suits, cartridge belts, shooting gloves, rare oriental carpets, cucumber sandwiches, leather-bound first editions, coin-silver snuff boxes . . .

Dreaming of these things, no doubt, has kept many an Englishman sane.

We did most of our getting about in those black London taxis built roomy enough to accommodate a gent in a top hat. The drivers always knew exactly where we were going; to qualify for a license, they spend at least two years traveling around the city on motorbikes acquiring "The Knowledge"—memorizing over 16,000 streets, landmarks, stores, restaurants, and other destinations in a 113-square-mile area. (Curious fact: The part of the human brain dedicated to spatial relationships grows significantly larger in London cabbies.) In the evenings we'd stroll the hushed back alleys of Kensington; if there'd been no cars, we could have been in 1900 or even 1850—but there were cars. Classic Bentleys, Jaguars, an occasional Vauxhall, even a 1920 Pierce-Arrow parked casually, its owner unafraid of crime.

All that magnificent machinery set me thinking. We were planning to visit Chartwell, Churchill's home; why hire a car with a driver, when we might rent something special on our own? So I told the desk clerk at Blakes that we'd like a Morgan roadster for a few days. "We'll get right on that, Mr. Peterman." Within two hours, the phone rang in my room. "Mr. Peterman, we've had the staff check every Morgan dealer and car-rental agency in London and we're unable to find a Morgan. The manager's brother owns a Morgan, though, and the manager is contacting him to see if it's available now."

As it turned out, the chap was out of the country. We never did get the car. But the effort that went into trying to fulfill my request was remarkable. Most hotels would have made a few calls and abandoned the search. Not Blakes.

———◆———

The Owner's Manual had a simple guarantee printed on the inside cover: "Absolute Satisfaction. Period." My Blakes' experience made me determined to live up to that guarantee. One time, Audrey marched into my office with a small army of customer-service reps, holding a pair of boots at arm's length. A customer had worn them out doing farm work, and he felt they should have lasted longer. He'd mailed them back to us for replacement, still covered with cow manure. The reps looked at me imploringly. These were dress boots, not intended for heavy-duty use. The man had gotten his money's worth. They were only defending the company's best interests.

It was a Big Moment. "We either have absolute satisfaction or we don't, " I said. "Ninety-nine-point-nine percent of our customers are honest. This man probably does feel the boots didn't hold up. If we send him another pair, he'll tell his friends about our great service. They'll become customers, too. That's the kind of company we want to be. That's the kind we're going to be."

We sent him new boots for free.

———◆———

People who achieve fame are usually brighter and more adventurous than average, whatever their public image. So I wasn't surprised when the catalog became an "inside thing" early on with celebrities—Nicole Kidman, Clint Eastwood, Tom Brokaw, Paul Newman and Joanne Woodward, Kim Basinger, Tom Hanks, Mia Farrow, Bill Murray, Angela Lansbury, and Sidney Pollack, among others. Once, as I was walking through our customer-service area with a venture capitalist, we happened to overhear a conversation. The VC's eyes widened. "Is that *the* Frank Sinatra on the phone?" he asked. I looked at the service rep's computer screen. "Well, his middle name *is* Albert."

We had a rule that any customer who wanted to talk to me should be put right through if I were available. I took an order that way from Kelly McGillis, who bought fireman's coats for herself and Jodie Foster. I felt shy about asking her bust size; being an actress, she wasn't a bit shy at all. I ended up as a sort of personal shopper for quite a few well-known people. One was Bill Simon, former secretary of the treasury. I used to spend time on the phone with him each November as he planned his holiday shopping. He liked to get my take on what different products were really like, whom they might suit, should he get this or that to furnish the house on his ranch? He didn't place orders with me; his secretary would call one of our service reps later. One time, though, he did ask me if he could get a discount on a big order. "Bill," I said, "when you were secretary of the treasury, did I get a discount?"

—◆—

Oprah Winfrey was one of our major fans, and when her producer called and asked if I would be on a show about catalog shopping, I didn't see how I could turn down such an excellent customer's request.

The drill was much as it had been when I was a plant doctor on *Good Morning America*. They sent me the airplane ticket, I flew to Chicago, was met by a limousine, taken to a good hotel, then whisked to Oprah's studio early next morning. They put me to work in the makeup room this time—I'd been asked to bring lots of possible items for models to wear, and I made up outfits on the spot to suit their looks. There was a fellow in charge of wardrobe who had his own ideas on how to dress the models, but because we were presenting Peterman, and I was Peterman, they ended up dressed the way I wanted.

I met Oprah when I joined her onstage. The program was in progress; they were at a commercial break. I walked on, shook her hand, and said, "I'm John Peterman," She smiled warmly. "No, you're J. Peterman . . . 'J.' is more mysterious." She turned to face the audience and the camera light blinked on.

Mostly, I just sat back and enjoyed the show. Oprah was a dynamo of enthusiasm. She swept here and there, picking up item after item, holding them out, putting them on, saying how the Owner's Manual was her favorite catalog, how she loved the copy, loved this dress, loved that coat, owned three of those shirts. She tried on several hats, turning around, asking the audience, "Isn't this great?" She put on the Shepheard's Hotel bathrobe and confided that it was the softest, most luscious robe and that she wore hers every morning.

The show ran just after Thanksgiving, and at the end of my segment they flashed our 800 number on the screen. Our incoming lines started to sizzle. The show aired first on the East Coast, and the volume of calls mounted in waves as it went on in successive time zones. Everyone in the company was manning the phones, scribbling orders on scraps of paper because our computer system was overtaxed. We managed to take about 25,000 calls in an atmosphere of pandemonium . . . then sudden silence.

Hurricane Oprah had crashed the Lexington, Kentucky, phone system.

*You can observe a lot just
by watchin'.*

—L. P. "Yogi" Berra (1925–   )

The Education
of John Peterman

You have an idea for a product or service (congratulations). You turn it over in your mind and find it's actually exciting enough for you to want to make it happen . . . at which point you quickly realize, if you hadn't known it already, that you won't get far by yourself. You need help from other people. Maybe just a few at the start, but if your idea takes off, there'll be 20, 30, 50, or more on that team of yours.

That's the position I found myself in with The J. Peterman Company. I didn't have an MBA degree. Couldn't afford to retain the services of a management consulting firm. I hadn't even read the mandatory biography of General George Patton. But there was one thing going for me:

I'd played a lot of baseball.

———————◆———————

I pulled a hamstring early in the season during my junior year at Holy Cross and was sidelined for the better part of a month. "Hop" Riopel picked a beefy sophomore second-stringer to cover third base in my absence. The kid was OK in the field—had an odd, clumsy way of catching grounders, but he did catch them, and when he threw to first it wasn't a rifle shot, but the ball got there. What made me edgy was how well he did at bat. The .275 average I'd earned the previous year was good, not great; now my replacement was churning out hard line drives, "frozen ropes," as we called them, two out of three times up.

I was looking on from the bench one day when he hit an impressive triple. I may have winced a bit, I don't know. Hop was walking by. "Take it easy, Peterman," he said in an off-hand aside, "your name's on third."

Hop wasn't being nice. Nice wasn't his style. The fact is, he'd carefully observed me catch, throw, hit, and push myself to make plays. He knew what I could deliver better than I did. He also knew that I and the rest of the team had already spent the whole previous season learning to mesh. He wasn't going to let a show of strong performance jeopardize the winning lineup he'd put together in his head, and he was right.

We made it to the College World Series that year, and the year after that.

Leadership, individual skill and drive, and teamwork combined to score is what the game's about off the field, too.

———◆———

The slugger mentality wasn't especially welcome in the Pittsburgh Pirates' "farm system"—the minor-league organization used to develop rookies like the young John Peterman for possible major-league play. Even the best big swings often miss, diminishing the chance for a big inning, and when the bat does connect, it often hits the bottom of the ball on an upstroke. That means lots of pop-ups, weak ground balls, and, if you're not built like a moose, easy flies into the outfield.

The Pittsburgh Theory of Hitting was different. We were taught to hit down on the top half of the ball, giving you a level swing at point of impact and reversing the spin to produce hard line drives that carry, or at least ground balls that have a chance of going through the infield for a base hit. And if that sounds a bit tame, let me remind you of Bill Mazeroski.

Bottom of the ninth in the decisive seventh game of the 1960 World Series at Forbes Field in Pittsburgh. It's the Pirates against the Yankees, score tied and the home team at bat.

Second-baseman Bill Mazeroski steps up to the plate. The pitcher feeds him his favorite food, a fastball. Putting Pittsburgh Theory into practice, Mazeroski drives it hard over left-fielder Yogi Berra's head, over the wall, winning the Series with what's been called the most dramatic home run in baseball history.

Mantle wept.

You learned to play ball the Pittsburgh way on the farm. You got to know your fellow players even better, sometimes, than you might have wanted to. And the Pittsburgh stories. You heard them over and over—not just about recent heroes like Bill Mazeroski and Roberto Clemente, but Honus Wagner, too, and did you know it was Pittsburgh, yes, Pittsburgh, that *invented* the idea of a World Series?

Coming from such a background, I felt it was the most natural thing in the world to have in-house training at The J. Peterman Company. Once people had proved themselves in the jobs they'd been hired for, they had the freedom to pursue whatever other avenues appealed to them. Paula Collins was the first of many employees to do that. I'd hired her as my catch-all assistant; she had previously been the secretary to a gentleman in White Plains, New York, who exported nuts and bolts. When she expressed an interest in sourcing, I began to let her watch the way I worked, took her along on nearby shopping expeditions, let her ask questions.

I'd explain to her why I picked this shirt instead of that one, or she'd choose something and I'd tell her why it did or didn't meet the criteria in my head. I have to applaud her patience; my tendency is to teach the way my dad did, just by doing, and expecting the other person to learn by osmosis. Eventually, though, it clicked. Paula emerged as one of the best merchants in the business, and more.

Out in the company on her own, she became a representative of our corporate culture, communicating to newer employees the things that made up the J. Peterman way: openness, initiative, freedom to make mistakes, and a spirit of mutual appreciation, in addition to opportunity for advancement. She shared the stories from the "early days" that helped to bind us together and talked up our success and recognition with enthusiasm. My investment in her was repaid many times over.

You can't get that with a "plug-in-the-resumé" approach to staffing.

It's a source of rueful pride that when the company went under, our employees, including those who'd been trained in-house by Audrey, Tom Holtzfcind, and others, as well as by me, generally went on to much higher-paying jobs at organizations ranging from Lands' End to the Smithsonian and the Metropolitan Museum of Art.

———◆———

Hop Riopel gave me an overview that proved invaluable when I became an ad hoc manager, but for one very important component I'm indebted to my high school baseball coach, Tony Gemma.

He was the opposite of the distant, rigid authority figure that was common in the 1950s, and still is, I suppose. You felt he expected good things from you. He never seemed to be holding back or working from some hidden agenda. In return, we felt at ease about going to him to bounce ideas around, get advice on our game, settle disputes, or confide personal problems. You went to Coach Gemma with the stuff that you didn't want to talk to your parents about—traffic tickets, girl trouble.

Fearless openness.

That's the atmosphere I tried to create, in a businesslike way, at The J. Peterman Company. My job as top manager went beyond directing and evaluating those who reported immediately to me. I wanted to motivate employees throughout the company, convince them I was a warm-blooded, straight-shooting, receptive human being—hence those Friday breakfasts in my office—and let them know my door was always open. I expected that to set the pattern down through other management positions. As a result, a surprising number of employees really did feel free to go to their managers with suggestions or problems, and if they didn't get a satisfactory hearing, they'd go to the next level, right on up to me.

Given good managers and mature employees, it's a self-fertilizing, self-weeding system that makes a more productive organization. It usually worked well for us. We never felt the need to invest in a human resources department, which all too often is a kind of off-to-the-side tank where discarded responsibilities fester.

———◆———

Some people will tell you that Willie Mays owns the greatest catch ever, but for my money the honor belongs to Roberto Clemente, and maybe several times over—like the amazing leaping, twisting snag he made against Mays himself at Forbes Field in 1960; his encounter with the right-field wall earned him seven glorious stitches on his chin.

You can't teach talent, of course, but you can encourage initiative. For as long as possible, I avoided writing down detailed job descriptions. Jobs were created around objectives that had to be met. "I'm going to tell you what we need to get done," I'd say. "You figure out how to do it." Most employees appreciated the trust put in them, showing an inventive, can-do attitude that worked miracles. It ordinarily takes six to nine months to create an edition of a catalog, from initial buying of items to the time it's in the mail; there were occasions when we achieved that in three months.

If you hear lots of discussions in your company about why such-and-such "can't be done," why it's "unaffordable," there's "not enough time," and so on, take a look at the rule book you've written; people may just be doing what they've been told.

———————◆———————

True corporate culture runs deeper than dispensing free latté and letting employees go barefoot. And true motivation is more than a generous stock option. I certainly believe in monetary rewards—I've often paid others more than I've paid myself—but they're no substitute for recognition of individual performance by management and fellow employees.

Before we installed a sophisticated computer system, it was difficult to crunch serious numbers, spot trends, analyze who was buying what when, or why items were being returned. So I was pleasantly surprised when a self-starter in the customer-service department went to Audrey and then came to me with the news that she'd found a common thread to the occasional incidents of credit-card fraud by customers.

"I was just curious at first," she said. "I started to look back through the orders, thought I saw a pattern. I kept track of new cases as they came up, and sure enough, there it was."

What was that?

"Well, look. Ashland, Kentucky; Danbury, Connecticut . . ."

Yes?

". . . Attica, New York; Soledad, California; Leavenworth, Kansas. John, our house mailing list has somehow incorporated a list for the U.S. prison system."

We were grateful for her discovery; it stopped a small problem from possibly becoming a costly major one. More important, we were grateful for the show of initiative. We made a point of publicly congratulating her for what she'd done, giving her a well-deserved lift, and energizing the rest of us, too. People talked about it in the halls, started looking for trends themselves, and frankly, I was motivated to finally bring our MIS out of the Stone Age.

———◆———

An away game for Holy Cross, with HC on the field. The other team has a man on second, and now the guy at bat knocks a hard single into right field. The first baseman moves into a direct line between the right fielder and the catcher to act as the "cutoff man," ideally positioned to either catch ("cut") the ball and relay or redirect if needed or else let it go on through to home, whatever it takes to nail the lead runner. Our right fielder, Hank, misses the cutoff man, however; the guy who was on second scores, and the hitter stretches one base into two.

Hank got chewed out for that one, and properly so. We'd been drilled over and over in all the varieties of cutoff plays. I can hear Hop Riopel now: "Hit the cutoff man! Hit the cutoff man! Hit the cutoff man!"

Anyone on your team who fouls up consistently on the basics deserves to be benched. No one would have criticized Clemente if he'd missed that impossible catch off Mays, though, and I never chewed out anyone at The J. Peterman Company for making mistakes in the course of learning or taking initiative. In fact, I was slightly suspicious of people who never seemed to make mistakes.

"If you don't make any mistakes, " I'd say, "you're probably not doing your job right."

When someone would come to me and say they'd fouled up, I'd reply, "OK. Now what are you going to do to fix it?" I made it clear that I didn't want anyone dumping problems on my desk without having thought through several solutions first. As a result, employees kept growing and doing better at their work, and they'd either resolve problems on their own or at least not be afraid to bring them to my attention while there was still time enough to do something about them.

————◆————

Notes written on yellowing 3″ × 5″ file cards found at the back of a drawer while cleaning out an office:

A mistake may turn out to be the one thing necessary to a worthwhile achievement.

—HENRY FORD (1863–1947)

Failures, repeated failures, are finger posts on the road to success. One fails forward toward success.

—C.F. KETTERING (1876–1958)

Success is 99 percent failure.

—SOICHIRO HONDA (1906–1991)

The man who makes no mistakes does not usually make anything.

—W.C. MAGEE (1821–1891)

The greatest mistake you can make in life is to be continually fearing you will make one.

—ELBERT HUBBARD (1859–1915)

Do not fear mistakes, there are none.

—MILES DAVIS (1926–1991)

———◆———

When you're running a business, it's important to think of your suppliers as part of the team, too. Spend time with them, develop relationships, and don't try to haggle them down to the last nickel. Our vendors were willing to cut us slack when we were strapped for cash back in 1989, before our first serious financing came through, because we'd always made deals that let both us and them walk away feeling happy.

I recall negotiating with Duke Gambert, the custom-shirt maker who produced our Gatsby Shirt. We wanted extremely fine fabric, to sell for about $60 a shirt. Duke did his calculations and told me that it wouldn't work. A quality shirt would have to sell for about $80 to give both of us our margins. Either that, use cheaper cloth, or go to another vendor. Well, we went with Duke, on his terms, and the shirts were exquisite, never a quality problem. We paid more than we had wanted to and we came out ahead.

We had good relations with our printer, Alden Press, right up until the last couple of years we were in business. Wonderful service, never missed a mailing date with them even if we were late in delivering catalog layouts. Then we started squeezing them on price, probably cut $100,000, maybe $150,000 out of a $10-million printing bill in a single year. That

Staley & me on a mission

John Rice & Audrey   Tom Holzfeind

Product development meeting, Oct. 31, 1997

Looking for new worlds to conquer

Peterman leads the charge

Early in the opium ceremony

I took the smallest room they had

Are my customers ready for this?

Negotiating with the Maharaja

My "loaner" from His Majesty

I can feel the asking price going up

Remembering who I forgot to be

On the road to Mandalay

Bedazzled again

Marshalling my forces on the Irrawaddy

My trunk & me on the E&O Express

I was too full to try the dried lizard

Graham Greene wrote here, too

A Peterman selection?

Katie Couric & her couturier

Will the real "J Peterman" stand up?

Early morning on the farm

Waldo & friend   *Ready to ride again*

looked like significant savings. But we created tension where none had existed before, and when we ran into trouble, they didn't pull for us. We weren't a partner anymore, just another sharp dealer.

It's an old saying about suppliers that's worth repeating: Good, fast, cheap; you can have any two out of three.

———————◆———————

I've been on teams where I was a star, and I've been on many more where I wasn't. Did I like being star? Absolutely. But there was something else I liked more. Winning. And you can't win with a bunch of stars, you can only win with a team. When George Steinbrenner first bought the Yankees, he signed on all the statistically best players; the team was a lineup of stars, but no one pulled together, and they didn't win much.

As of this writing, the Yankees under Joe Torre have become winners again, recalling the Casey Stengel era. ("It's easy to get the players," said Professor Stengel. "It's getting them to play together that's the hard part.") The Yankees expect to win every time they go to the ballpark. That attitude is a direct by-product of a supportive culture, the feeling that everyone contributes and that the result will be positive.

117

I might have a bad day, you might have a bad day, but that's OK; I'll come through for you on your bad day, and you'll come through for me on mine.

———◆———

"Talent is what drives the company forward," Don said. "Talent is the only thing that counts."

"Don," I said, "without the team, talent just sits in a room making marks on pieces of paper that nobody else in the world is ever going to see."

———◆———

The merchant was standing in front of my desk bristling, her back ramrod straight, barely able to keep silent. She held out a large leather-bound volume with her name embossed on it in gold, waiting for me to take it. A portfolio of her work, all the products she'd had a hand in.

"What's up?" I asked her after I finished leafing through the pages.

"I think I deserve a raise. A substantial one. All those products are mine. A lot of them are best-sellers."

"It's an impressive collection."

"Thank you. I think it proves I should be making more than anyone else."

"You probably do deserve more money," I said. "You have very good ideas. But look, this dress, didn't so-and-so suggest this collar change to the one you brought in? This spread of hats, weren't two or three of these found by other merchants? You don't really mean to say that everything in these pages is absolutely, positively 100% yours, do you?"

"I suppose not."

"Good," I said, warming to the subject. "You know, your success is our success, and vice versa. Even if everyone here does a magnificent job, from having a product idea through designing, picking a vendor, manufacturing, marketing, copy-writing, illustrating, printing, and mailing, and then the guy filling the order packs the wrong thing in the box, why, we're all losers."

After putting her through that, I had to give her the raise.

———◆———

There was a premium on creativity in many areas at The J. Peterman Company, room for lots of stars to show what they could do. The grown-up talents had a realistic way of looking at things. They knew that we are all tools of each other's ambition, to be used with mutual respect.

Unfortunately, you'll find that not all talented people are especially grown-up.

Underneath a charming and confident exterior, often there's a core of insecurity, and they don't seem to believe that other human beings exist in the same way they do. Anything that suggests they're not sufficiently appreciated or agreed with, any perceived threat to their control, and they're likely to go into a sulk or a Vesuvius of rage.

I once told a merchant to prepare a graphic guide to help our purchasing and inventory people, assigning amounts of space to products based on their projected sales—a best-seller would get a page, a so-so item maybe a quarter of a page, and so on; I figured that would be easier to understand than mere columns of numbers alone. Well, a creative got wind of it and leaped to the conclusion that it was an actual catalog layout designed to end-run his responsibility. He gave the merchant a furious tongue-lashing, calling her a "talentless hack" who was going to "screw up everything."

She came into my office, closed the door, and burst into tears. Totally demoralized.

It took 15 minutes to get a rough account of what had happened. When she seemed more or less collected, I asked about one point that puzzled me: Did she tell the person that I was the one who had instructed her to do the job? Yes, she replied, but that didn't have any effect; it was as if her critic actually enjoyed erupting at her.

The least attractive feature of some talents is the way they make good people feel bad about themselves.

———◆———

I always tried to be patient with cocky younger talent; the minors are full of guys who naturally outplayed everyone else when they were growing up, but keep missing the cutoff man. My hope was that over time, our corporate culture would wear away their attitude and their abilities would round out, mature, to give them real inner confidence.

Then there were the tougher cases, including that irate creative who felt so free to vent. What can you do with them?

Sometimes they unintentionally solve things by themselves. Their abrasive style alienates everyone so much that nobody wants anything to do with them, and they get cut out of the loop. This may sound cynical, but if they choose to stay on and you choose to let them, you've got a sort of genie in a bottle there to consult as needed, and they may even be grateful for it.

Other talents are relatively cool-headed, calculating, political types. They may attract admirers around them to form cliques and spread rumors—I've been the target of some beauties over the years. My policy was always to maintain a disinfecting openness, encourage a spirit of unity (company celebrations, unified offices, etc.), and, if necessary, invite the party into my office for what diplomats call "a frank exchange of views."

As a rule, ask yourself: Does this person's contribution outweigh the damage he does sufficiently for you to tolerate him? That's a difficult one—like asking how many home runs a slugger has to produce for you to tolerate casual jogs to first on easy pop-ups when everyone else has to really run the ball out. So much resentment may build up, in spite of your efforts to get the other players to swallow a double standard, that it might be best for you to invite the slugger off the team in any case.

Expect to make your share of bad calls.

———◆———

Some postmortem critics have said that The J. Peterman Company's open culture allowed too much freedom and that freedom was a critical factor in our demise. Not true. There's ample evidence of very large companies that have an open, nurturing, nondictatorial atmosphere—just as there are plenty of smaller ones whose managers seem to have trained with the Gestapo. A favorite technique of retail management, for example, is to show up at a store unannounced, decide some detail is wrong, demand that the person responsible step forward, and then fire him on the spot, ensuring that fear runs through the company.

Of course, an organizational structure that works for a $10-million business isn't going to suit a $100-million operation. As you grow, you have to create new functions, new paths of reporting, and tighter job definitions to avoid people tripping over each other or poaching each other's work. The trick is to design your start-up in a way that anticipates the need to evolve instead of resisting it, without risking your core cultural values.

Take that from someone who learned the hard way.

One cannot change the size or quantity of anything without changing its quality.

—P. Valéry (1871–1945)

Seinfeld and Me

April 18, 1995. "J. Peterman" debuts on America's most popular TV show without me knowing a thing about it. The program aired while I was flying back from San Francisco, and when I got to the office next morning I was greeted with excitement.

"You were on *Seinfeld* last night, didn't you see it?"

"You hired Elaine to work here as a writer!"

"Are they going to put you on again?"

Someone gave me a tape of the show to watch. It was a funny episode. The amazingly self-centered Elaine Benes is at the beauty parlor and learns that her Korean manicurist is making rude remarks about her in Korean to the other giggling beauticians, right in front of her face. She's crushed. As she stumbles through the rainy streets, sobbing, she bumps into a tall, distinguished gent:

ELAINE: *Oh, oh God, I'm so sorry. I don't even know where I'm going.*

GENT: *That's the best way to get somewhere you've never been.*

ELAINE: *Yeah, I suppose that's true.*

GENT: *Have you been crying?*

ELAINE: *Yeah, you see, this woman, this manicurist . . .*

GENT: *Oh no, no. It doesn't matter why. That's a very nice jacket.*

ELAINE: *(cheering up at the attention): Oh, thanks.*

GENT: *Very soft. Huge button flaps. Cargo pockets. Drawstring waist. Deep bi-swing vents in the back. Perfect for jumping into a gondola.*

ELAINE: *How do you know all that?*

GENT: *That's my coat.*

ELAINE: *You mean . . .*

GENT: *Yes. I'm J. Peterman.*

———◆———

I thought we came off pretty well, all things considered. It was kind of flattering that the *Seinfeld* people felt J. Peterman was interesting enough to create a character around. And

I didn't mind the fact that our name was being publicized for free to nearly 40 million viewers.

A couple of weeks later I got a call from the show's producer. *Seinfeld* had recently spoofed someone—the dictatorial owner of a gourmet take-out soup shop in New York City, whom they dubbed "the Soup Nazi"—and he had sued. Would I mind giving my approval to future Peterman scripts? Glad to oblige. I began receiving scripts about six weeks in advance; I would just sign off on them and send them back. Never changed a comma.

Any resemblance between the plots and what really went on in the J. Peterman Company was purely coincidental. One show had Elaine acquiring JFK's golf clubs at auction; we were in fact at that auction, at Sotheby's, but we passed on the clubs. (Arnold Schwartzenegger picked them up for a mere $772,500.) Another time, Peterman was going to Burma ("You most likely know it as Myanmar") for a secluded nervous breakdown; I *had* been to Burma, and was traveling through a remote area of China when the show aired, but I was just shopping.

Previewing scripts came in handy once when my sister called to tell me to turn on NBC, I was on the show again. My mother was staying with her; was she watching too? "Yes," Sis replied. "Well, sit close to her," I said. "She dies in this episode."

My daughter, who happens to be an actress, auditioned for *Seinfeld* after the Peterman character had been on for a while. When Jerry Seinfeld asked her name, she said, "Robyn Peterman." "Yeah, sure," he replied, "and I suppose you're going to tell me that your father is J. Peterman." She didn't take the part; by chance, though, she did play a lead in *Sour Grapes*, the first movie written by Larry David, the co-creator of *Seinfeld*.

I developed a friendship with John O'Hurley, the dashing, mellow-voiced veteran TV actor who played Peterman; he'd send me wine, and I'd send him clothes. Sometimes the *Seinfeld* people would ask us for clothing and furnishings to use as props, and items we were selling would wind up on the show. The Owner's Manual gave us a chance to tease them back, now and then, as in a piece entitled "Dear Elaine":

> *Thank you for giving up your weekend to search Yogyakarta for a really authentic batik caftan. Not everyone has the dedication to ride around during thunderstorms in an open pedicab. . . . $12 for a face and neck massage in Yogya is perfectly reasonable. Just send me the receipt.*

Fair is fair.

———◆———

So The J. Peterman Company became a national fixture. That was fine with me. I had great confidence in the potential of the Peterman concept. If we could double sales from the $45 million we'd had in 1992, we'd gain all kinds of profitable efficiences in our operations and in the deals and prices we could get from suppliers. In the back of my mind I was also thinking of our investors; they weren't anxious or making demands, but venture capitalists want to see a good tenfold return on their money within three to five years.

We were adding so many new products from 1993 on that editions of the Owner's Manual often came out in two volumes. We increased the frequency of mailings. We tested more and more lists in our search for new customers. All that entailed growth—and change—in every area of the company.

There were more merchants and writers to hire, train, and manage. And we had to formalize the way we gave thumbs up or down to products for the catalogs. During the first years of the company, I used to meet with merchants to go over products anytime, anywhere; now we were all so busy that the process couldn't be casual. We introduced "cull meetings," where everyone would bring in items and we'd sit around in a big room and go over them, one by one, accepting them, rejecting them, tweaking them—"Is this unique? Does it have some factual romance? Would it be better with wooden buttons?" Eventually we held five or six cull meetings a year, each lasting three or four days, from early morning until late at night, or until everybody was so cranky from caffeine that we couldn't go on.

The cull meetings created some unhealthy office politics. I would still look at products informally, all the time, just as I kept the final say on products as well as merchants. But now, people would show me things privately to get input so they'd have a leg up in the meeting, or they'd stop me in the hallway to show me one item from a trip but hold back something else that they thought was really the find of the day. Sometimes they'd go to Don first, to get his support for a product before bringing it in. Then, if I was on the fence about it, it would be, "Dad says 'No,' but Uncle Don says 'Yes.' "

We made a host of costly but essential operational changes, too, updating phone systems, computers, software. We weathered several bank mergers, building relationships with new loan officers each time, keeping finances on track. And we moved again. On Palumbo Drive, we'd expanded to the point where merchants and marketing people were in one office building, with me, while customer service, accounting, and MIS were in another building across the driveway; the warehouse people were scattered through four other buildings. It was getting hard to communicate, and an "us-versus-them" mentality started to develop. I wanted to avoid that kind of atmosphere, so in early 1995 we relocated to a site on Russell

Cave Road, with offices and a 100,000-square-foot warehouse all under one unifying roof.

We moved the entire company over a single weekend. On Friday night, half the customer service staff was at Palumbo Drive and half was at Russell Cave Road; we just threw a switch at midnight and calls were directed to the new offices. We were shipping on Friday and shipping on Monday.

Customer service was at the heart of our business; we never missed a beat when it came to that.

———◆———

PETERMAN EMPLOYEE: *(reading catalog copy he has written): So I pressed through the rushes, and there below me were the shining waters of Lake Victoria . . .*

JP: *Oh, for the love of God, man, just tell me what the product is.*

EMPLOYEE: *It's a washcloth.*

JP: *No washcloths!*

ELAINE: *Well, Mr. Peterman, I've got a really good idea for a hat. It combines the spirit of old Mexico with a little big-city panache. I like to call it the "Urban Sombrero."*

JP: *(looking pained, rubbing his neck): Oh, my neck is one gargantuan monkey fist.*

131

ELAINE: *Are you OK, Mr. Peterman?*

JP: *Yes, yes, go on, go on, go on.*

ELAINE: *Well, see, it's businessmen taking siestas. It's the Urban Sombrero (Peterman leaves the room, groaning) . . . Mr. Peterman?*

———◆———

You might think merchants have a glamorous life, jetting to exotic destinations, wining and dining on the cuff, merrily shopping. The reality is otherwise. They work hard from early in the morning until late at night, constantly juggling the need to search around for new sources with the need to be as productive as possible. They're on a schedule, after all, and they're expected to bring back the goods. It's a kind of risk management; "I got this great tip, and I probably should rent a car, take an afternoon, follow it up, but it might not play out, and then that's a whole afternoon wasted. If I stay in town, I know I'll find something."

I always encouraged our merchants to venture off the beaten path, and also experience local culture—bangers and the Tate in London, snails and the Eiffel Tower in Paris—to get a contextual feeling for what they were buying. Still, when you've done a city several times you inevitably tend to slip into a routine, emerging from your favorite hotel to shop your favorite haunts. By 1993, I felt we were getting too comfortable on our trips to Europe. It was time for us to break new ground.

I called Tom Evans, an old friend who'd been a catcher with me in the minors and was now semi-retired in Delhi. I told him I wanted to open up India; would he help make arrangements at that end? Tom is the kind of guy who'd say "Great, I'm ready" if you suggested a mission to Mars. In three weeks, I had my tickets and he'd booked my hotel and made appointments for me with Indian purchasing agents and vendors.

After a 23-hour trip from Atlanta to Delhi by way of Frankfurt, I found myself on the long customs line at Indira Gandhi International Airport. Early morning, already hot and crowded. I observed a sign in English listing the countries for which India requires a visa; oops, my travel agent overlooked that little detail. When I got to the counter, the customs official rolled his eyes and pointed to a corner: "Sir, you must please stand there." Eventually, I was told I had 48 hours to obtain a visa at the Foreigners Registration Office. I thought 48 hours was generous, but it took me the entire next day to get the paperwork done, going from one line to another and back again, over and over. It was a small taste of Indian bureaucracy—I understand that a gent in Poona recently won a court case filed by his ancestors over 750 years ago.

When I finally escaped airport customs, there was Tom, waiting patiently, in much better spirits than I was; some of the Indian sense of fatalism had rubbed off on him. We climbed into an Indian-made two-door that looked like a Chevy Blazer and put ourselves into the hands of our driver, Rajit, for one of the more riveting rides of my life.

The basic rule of the road in India is that might makes right—the bigger your vehicle and the louder your horn, the better. Within minutes of leaving the airport we were practically run over by an insistently honking truck with a four-armed Hindu god painted on it in bright, garish colors. Rajit swerved onto the dirt shoulder to let it roar by and then back onto the road, without braking or slowing down. During our ride I counted five crashed cars and three crashed trucks, one still burning, plus an overturned bullock cart, dead bullock attached. As we pulled up at the hotel, Rajit flashed a brilliant smile at us:

"Very fine motorway conditions today, it is a sign of luck."

The hotel was a big, modern affair called the Oberoi; it would have been at home in any major city around the world. I usually try to stay at small, special places with local flavor, but Tom advised me not to be adventurous with Indian lodging or food. It was excellent advice, right up there with Don't Drink the Water, and Remember that Ice Cubes Are Water, Too.

Tom was my guide during the whole trip, and after I left, he became our follow-up contact, working with the Indian vendors and manufacturers. What I was doing, essentially, was establishing a ground network, so that when I returned, or when other merchants went there, we'd have a home base from which to ferret out the good stuff. Without such a base, foreign countries are overwhelming—particularly India, which has the most of everything, from poverty and ugliness to opulence and beauty.

———◆———

JP: (at dinner with George Costanza): And there, tucked into the river's bend, was the object of my search. The Chiang Mai river market. Fabrics and spices traded under a starlit sky. It was there that I discovered the Pamplona Beret. Sizes 7-1/2 to 8-3/4. Price, $35.
GEORGE: How about sports? You follow sports?

———◆———

Everything looks wonderful at the start of a buying trip, especially when you're in a new country surrounded by unfamilar products. Under no circumstances should you buy anything on the first day; often as not, you find yourself wishing there were some way to return it.

My initial week in India was devoted purely to scouting activity. I recall one early visit to a small shop filled with gleaming navigational equipment, compasses, telescopes; there was a tang of brass in the air that made your mouth water. I examined a hefty surveyor's level of 19th-century design, the kind the Brits employed to carve up East Africa and lay railroad tracks throughout India.

"Is this original?" I asked the shopkeeper.

"Original, sir, no problem."

I pointed to a handsome sextant that might have been used by Captain Cook to plot a course for the *Endeavour*. "Is that original, too?"

"It is all original, sir."

Through a partly drawn curtain at the rear of the store, I could see a wizened old man assembling brass parts to create more sextants; from an Indian point of view, I suppose, that may well have made them "original."

Later, I met the Mehra brothers, Sushil, Mirah, and Yunis, and spent days inspecting the treasure trove at their wonderful "art farm" outside Delhi. The grounds and several big barns were stocked with acres of British colonial furniture, ethnic handicrafts, temple doors and columns, elaborately carved dugout canoes, gods, goddesses, and erotic nymphs in stone, wood, and bronze, to name a few items. They appeared to date from the ninth to the 19th centuries, but the brothers were up front with me: most were actually skillful contemporary reproductions.

"Export of anything more than 100 years old is illegal," said Mirah. "All our antiques have been declared nonantiques by the Archaeological Survey."

The Mehra brothers ultimately did a lot of work with us. Among other things, they became our primary supplier of oriental rugs. They were on my wavelength for quality and selection, and usually quite reliable, although once, Tom sent me an alarming fax. "The rugs will be late," it said. "Yunis has them, and he has been kidnapped in Kashmir." His father had to pay 10,000 rupees and a used Jeep to ransom him. Being the conscientious fellow he was, Yunis made sure the rugs were ransomed, too.

We had our share of difficulties with Indian vendors, like the case of the mahogany cash boxes. Very nice boxes, with beautiful brass fittings. I'd asked that they be "clean" when they were shipped to us, and when we opened the crates in Lexington, we found that to someone in India, "clean" had meant, "Scour the brass fittings with steel wool until they are thoroughly scratched."

Misunderstandings like that are common between U.S. companies and their foreign suppliers. American managers try to fix the problems from afar, flooding the overseas people with information, when the real solution is for someone from the home company to observe the situation firsthand and demonstrate how they want things done.

A product-development person once complained to me, "The shirt maker in Ecuador is hopeless, the sizes are all off." I looked at the reams of technical information she was sending; the specs were in inches instead of centimeters. "We don't have a quality problem, " I said, "we have a communication gap." I took her along on my next trip to South America, had her speak directly with the factory boss, and everything was resolved in one meeting. You could see the light bulb switch on over her head.

India became a great success for us. We sold lots of colonial furniture and brass instruments (clearly noted as reproductions, if they were), as well as kilims, quilts, and caftans, Tibetan shaman jackets, elegant angami beads from Ao and Lhota. We were being closely watched by other catalogs, though; it was startling how quickly similar items often appeared in their pages.

———◆———

PETERMAN EMPLOYEE: *(on hearing that Elaine is going to run the catalog in Peterman's absence): You're taking the job?*

ELAINE: *You got that straight. Now I want four new ideas from each of you by 6 o'clock. No. Make that six ideas by 4 o'clock. All right. Let's Move! Move! Move! Move! Move!*

———◆———

There was scarcely a spot on the planet or a period in history that The J. Peterman Company didn't explore, from India to Bozeman, Montana, from Victorian England to the Alexandrian Empire. And yet, finding new products gradually became more of a chore than an adventure, with the catalog driving the merchants instead of the other way around. There was less time to discover that one special thing. "Hey, look at this wonderful jacket I found" was becoming, "Get out of my way, I need to turn up twenty more items by the end of the week."

Predictably, some humdrum items began to appear. The catalog would make them as intriguing as honestly possible, but that increased the risk of disappointing customers who had come to expect the best. Our first five or six years of operation saw a low rate of orders returned for refund or exchange, seldom more than 20%. Now, return rates were as high as 50%.

(To be fair, the highest returns were usually on women's fitted dresses and blouses; in earlier days, much of our clothing was unstructured, generously sized stuff, like the simple pima-cotton women's nightshirt we romanced as "What Marie-Antoinette wore to bed.")

Harried merchants were less careful about filling out the "fact sheets" that gave the writers product information to work with. Instead of pinpointing the place and era that something came from, providing details on materials and workmanship, factual reasons it was unique and authentic, they'd dash off comments like, "I bought this in England because it's romantic." Attitude without substance.

Even under ideal circumstances, it could take a day or two to craft a good piece of Owner's Manual copy. Now, writers were under the gun to produce. Unfortunately, there weren't many who could turn out the literate, inventive work we wanted, consistently, and in one voice. Despite their best efforts, editing right up to the deadlines, Don and Bill couldn't keep all of it in hand.

More artwork was needed than Bob Hagel could do by himself, so we hired more artists, too. Some were acceptable, some were problematic. One lady illustrator tended to make women's skirts and pants legs abnormally long, like the ones in drawings for conventional department-store ads, and there was a fellow who couldn't resist endowing men's trousers with inappropriate bulges. Sometimes art like that would arrive just in time to meet the production schedule; we'd be locked into using it.

Matters weren't helped when the cost of the paperstock that we printed the Owner's Manual on went up 40% in 1995.

Price hikes for paper (and postage) are "acts of God" that have wiped out many a mail-order company. The only thing to do was to switch to cheaper, thinner paper, even though it didn't have the same feel of quality to the touch, and it let type and images show through from the other side of a page, giving the catalog a slightly dingy look.

It was almost as if we were becoming a diluted version of what we'd been.

———◆———

VOICE ON INTERCOM: *Mr. Peterman on line one.*
ELAINE: *Hello, Mr. Peterman, how are you feeling?*
JP: *Elaine, I'll be blunt. I'm burnt out. I'm fried. My mind is as barren as the surface of the moon.*

———◆———

By the airdate of J. Peterman on *Seinfeld*, all observers agreed that the company was on top of the world. Sometimes it felt that way to me, too. Sometimes it didn't. Trying to keep merchants, writers, and artists on track could be like herding cats. I found myself spending more hours than I would have liked listening to grievances, cooling down squabbles, resolving issues that should have been decided by others.

In the evening, when everyone had cleared out of my office, I'd lean back in my chair, put my boots up on the desk, and stare into space, looking for patterns. Sales had continued upwards, from $45 million in 1992 to $62 million in 1994, but that was half the growth rate we'd enjoyed before. And our profitability was down. You could explain some of it by increased costs of overhead, staff, paper, and postage. Still . . .

If I'd been a Merlin of Mail-Order, I'd have realized we were approaching the limits of our effectiveness as a catalog operation. We'd been running direct-response print ads and testing mailing lists for quite a while. Speaking generally, you can reach about a quarter of your potential customers with a catalog proposition, because that's the percentage of the population that likes to buy through catalogs in the first place. Moreover, most of your sales will come from 25% or less of those who actually buy something. Over time, the more you spend on bigger catalog mailings, the less results you tend to get per catalog.

I'm not sure I'd have been receptive right then to such a bracing appraisal. Besides, Don was convinced he had the answer. "If 5% of the people we mail to are buying from us, that means 95% aren't," he'd say. "We need to put more products in the catalog to appeal to more of them." He suggested that we merchandise products in outfits, rather than individually. That's what we did, starting in the fall 1995 Owner's Manual—even though it increased product proliferation and made for cluttered pages.

Don could be persuasive, especially to someone who was already inclined to be persuaded.

———◆———

We used to hold weekly marketing meetings to review response rates for the catalog, each edition of which was mailed out in stages over the course of a month or so. We'd compare results with past response, go over sales figures for individual items, make forecasts.

The meeting was tense when results for the fall of 1995 came in.

John Rice and I sat at my poker table with Jonathan, our circulation manager, and Katie, the head of marketing. The numbers weren't good. Sales were very soft. Slow sales meant we'd end up with too much inventory on hand. Too much inventory meant we'd be strapped for cash.

"Holidays are coming up, our best season," someone said optimistically. "The holiday catalog could turn things around."

"Don't count on it," I said. "This business is about trends, and we're in a bad trend."

John nodded. "Retailers are getting ready for a weak Christmas," he said. "Consumer confidence is down—flat wages, high debt, all those headlines about corporate downsizing. Shoppers will be looking for bargains this year."

"What about mailing deeper into the J. Crew list?"

We dismissed that one. In order to prospect for customers you can add to your own house mailing list, you rent lists from other catalogs and start by mailing to the most recent, biggest-spending buyers, then relax your criteria to go "deeper" into the list. When trends are bad, though, mailing deeper is just digging a deeper hole. You can't "mail your way out."

I stared into my third cup of coffee. "Well, there's Japan," I said.

"Right," Jonathan said. "The guy in Tokyo who ordered 2,000 dusters."

It was true. We'd had a following in Japan since 1988, when a mysterious gentleman bought 2,000 dusters. Lots of Japanese had requested the catalog since then, on their own, without us spending a nickle on marketing. We were doing well over a million dollars' worth of business there a year. It cost about $4 to mail a catalog to Japan, versus $1 in the U.S., but the Japanese were "high-dollar" customers; while each U.S. catalog made $5 in sales, on average, the Japanese figure was $30—and there were never any returns.

Katie spoke up. She was concerned. "It's hard to get a clean mailing list for Japan, John," she said. "A lot of the addresses aren't accurate."

"I hear you. But even if we do only $10 a book, where's the problem?"

I made the call. Operation Rising Sun began.

The nature of war certainly does not let us see at all times where we are going.

—K. von Clausewitz (1780–1831)

Why Generals Have
Their Own Tents

Flying north over Bluegrass Country on a clear morning at 2,500 feet in my single-engine Cessna. The Kentucky River coming up, winding around Lexington through high limestone palisades that hide the water itself from your view until you're directly over it, yes, there it is, a narrow ribbon of quicksilver that flashes briefly, then is gone.

I can see the roofing of The J. Peterman Company off to the right now, a flat black chip a quarter the size of a postage stamp. Audrey is down there, I imagine, giving customer service reps the daily pep talk. John Rice is crunching numbers. Doug is loading orders onto the UPS trucks.

Glance at the fuel gauge. I could make it to Kansas City by lunchtime for barbecue. I could make it to Ontario, disappear forever into the woods.

I continue on instead to the landing strip at Blue Grass Airport ("One of the finest airports found in any city of any size," said Capt. Eddie Rickenbacker). In half an hour, I'm at my desk.

———◆———

We'd been right not to mail deeper into our rented lists during the 1995 holidays. Catalog companies and retail stores had the worst sales that season since the 1990 recession. Even discounters were stuck with unsold inventory. But my Operation Rising Sun was a disaster, too; it ended up adding another $400,000 to our loss for the year.

Not surprising, in hindsight. Our Japanese business had all come from customers who were self-selected, who'd made a special personal effort to get catalogs. "Highly-qualified prospects," as direct-marketers say. A similar group of Americans would also be abnormally good customers. You can't logically project broader results based on experience with such groups.

I'd made a hasty, bad decision in the heat of battle, like a soldier who doesn't think beyond "How do I get out of this gunfire?" Generals are supposed to have some distance from the front lines. They're supposed to be relatively calm and collected, high on a hill, so they can see where the fire is coming from, appraise what's likely to happen next, check their resources, and devise effective tactics that don't compromise overall strategy.

I should have paid more attention to a piece in the Owner's Manual, entitled "Let's Talk About Your Career":

> *A lucky man starts out doing what he loves. He does it well enough to prosper. Eventually, though, he finds that what he loves has become just a small part of what he has to do.*
>
> *He accumulates dark suits . . . starts getting testy.*
>
> *Are you at (or nearing) this danger point? I'd suggest making this sporty Italian blazer part of your life.*
>
> *Wearing it feels like opening all the windows in a corner office and letting the papers blow off the desk. Encourages you to get out on the links more often, spend a month around Lake Como, think about what really matters: delegation, and Where We Want to Be Five Years from Now . . .*

———◆———

In the late 1980s and early 1990s, flying had been an important way to keep myself fresh for the job. I always landed feeling renewed, better able to handle my responsibilities as entrepreneur, top manager, father, husband, horseman, or whatever else was on the menu.

I'd dreamed of flying since the summer I turned 16. My family had left for a two-week vacation on Cape Cod without me—I'd had a baseball game I didn't want to miss—and my father chartered a small plane to bring me and a friend up to Barnstable after the game; that was affordable then. It was my first time in the air. I flipped a coin with my friend, he got the co-pilot's seat, and I was in the back, but it didn't matter. I watched the pilot concentrate, marveled at all the dials and knobs and switches; looking out the window, I imagined how wonderful it must be to fly alone, away from everything.

Soon after starting The J. Peterman Company, I decided it was time. Drove out to Blue Grass and walked across the tarmac to the flight-school office located in a hangar that housed private planes. "How do I sign up for flying lessons?" I asked. Within 15 minutes, I was at the controls of a Cessna 152, an instructor seated next to me.

Most of learning to fly is earthbound, at first, in the class-room. You have blocks of half an hour or so in the air to start and work your way up to longer periods as you progress. When you're doing those short flights, you get noticeably better each day. I moved rapidly through the lessons with my instructor, gaining the basics and racking up the hours I needed to solo.

Soloing is quite different from flying with a seasoned hand to back you up. Actions that felt almost effortless when the instructor was with me took on extreme significance, and rightly so. One wrong lever flipped, one misjudgment, and you have an excellent chance of killing yourself. "The day you stop concentrating," my instructor said, "is the day you should quit."

The first few times I went up by myself, I was tense, nervous, and I had more concentration than I'd ever marshalled before; baseball isn't actually a life-or-death matter. I focused intently on what needed to be done at each exact moment, emptying my mind of all else. Later, I learned to loosen up, but I still gave total concentration.

Flying is something you must practice all the time if you want to be good at it. You have to develop your skills constantly. Every second spent figuring out what to do when the inevitable emergencies arise is flirting with eternity. By the time I had close to 200 hours in the air, though, I was flying less often than I would have liked.

This was going to be a routine hour-and-a-half solo from Lexington to southern Indiana, in a plane rented from the flight school. Took off just after breakfast. I'd checked the weather at my destination, done everything else I should have. The field I planned to land at was "uncontrolled"; there was no one in a tower to bring me in, but it had a manned radio whose frequency was printed in my flight manual, and that's all I needed.

When I approached the landing field and tuned into the frequency, I got dead air. I rechecked the manual; it was up-to-date, so I tried again. Nothing. OK, then, let's look for other planes, get into the pattern, and land. Hmm, no planes in sight, must be a slow day. Well, the last report said the wind was from the north, let's approach from the south and get positioned for a proper landing into the wind.

What I should have done was fly over the field for a con-firming look at the wind sock. I realized that as I got into my final approach and started to have problems bringing the plane down with a tailwind boosting me. Then, when I was about 100 feet off the ground, in slow, full-flaps-down descent, I saw a plane that must have been revving incon-spicuously on the taxiway a minute before heading straight toward me on the runway for takeoff; it probably hadn't occurred to the pilot that someone would actually try to land with the wind. I needed to get out of the way. I couldn't just speed up and raise my flaps fully to ascend, though; in my current situation, that would actually cost me a fatal 100 feet or so of altitude first.

I gave the plane full throttle and began a coordinated right turn, raising the flaps just enough to start ascending.

I landed safely. The other guy took off fine. The return trip was uneventful. But that was my last flight as a pilot. I'd have to find a different way to recharge my batteries.

———◆———

The consequences of a single pilot error are very quickly and dramatically apparent. It's seldom like that when you're operating a business. Errors in judgment accumulate over time, almost imperceptibly, until one day you realize that your thrilling ride is actually a hazardous runaway situation.

In 1993, a merchant came to a cull meeting with an assortment of casual coordinated tops and bottoms for women, well-made items in a soft fabric we called "cotton cashmere," but basically a sweatsuit look. Nothing unique or hard to find, not a shred of factual romance.

The merchant argued at length. Just give them one chance, she begged. Peterman blinked. We ran a spread with highly empathetic copy about balancing work and life, desire and reality, and it pulled in a phenomenal $300,000 in orders. The stuff was in the Owner's Manual for keeps after that, powerful support for other departures from the essence of the brand.

I might have thought harder before saying "yes" if I'd kept up my flying.

———◆———

Our "cotton cashmere" had what might be taken as a precedent—a best-selling spread of dressier coordinated skirts, pants, dresses, vests, sweaters. Just two differences: the earlier collection was exclusive Italian design, executed in luxurious Italian Merino wool.

The Italians have a gift for creating something wonderful out of practically nothing, and drawing attention without creating a spectacle. They like it to look easy; it's hard work, actually. We ran a piece once, "The Agony and The Ecstasy," that touched on the subject:

> *Rome. Metropolis of Michelangelo and Bernini.*
>
> *In a market, Giancarlo spends 20 minutes selecting the perfect . . . eggplant.*
>
> *"Americans are fortunate," he says, tossing one that looks fine to me back into the bin. "They can ignore the past. But who," he waves out toward The Eternal City with some irritation, "who can ignore all that? Aha!"*
>
> *His shoulders straighten as he picks out a likely specimen, and then heads for the pasta section with a noticeably lighter step.*

My own real-life Giancarlo was Guido Mazzoli, our purchasing agent in Italy. Guido is a perfectionist when it comes to his job, never a lapse in taste or shrewdness. I think that may be partly due to his insistence on balancing work with a thoughtful enjoyment of the good things in life.

I learned from him; I wish I'd made time to learn more.

Guido once invited Audrey and me and a small group of friends to a restaurant named Cupoli, just outside the Tuscan town of Lastra a Signa. It took us half an hour to drive the five miles from Florence through heavy initial traffic, then up the narrow, winding roads that rise away from the city. Our destination proved to be a hilltop villa with a back courtyard made up of several walled terraces stepping down the slope. The owner is Rosanna Piombini, a talented sommelier; curiously, she never actually drinks wine, but her taste (and Guido's) is impeccable.

It was dusk when we arrived. August, the air clear and balmy. Rosanna escorted us to one of the lower terraces, seating us on stone benches at a stone table, under a vine-covered pergola; off there in the valley, past the vineyards and olive groves, the city lights were beginning to glitter.

She brought welcoming loaves of schiacciata, served with local virgin olive oil, Italy's best, and our first wine of the evening. Our waiter appeared, looking expectantly at Guido, smiling at the rest of us, ready to engage.

The two of them got into a discussion that lasted 10 minutes. I knew Guido was ordering dinner, but sometimes he and the waiter seemed to be arguing the merits of opposing soccer teams; a few moments later, they'd appear to be agreeing on a fine point of theology. Neither of them consulted the rest of us, there was no, "Can you eat butter?" or "How do you like yours done?" This was Guido's meal; he and the waiter and the chef and Rosanna were collaborating on a work of artful simplicity.

Crostini emerged with a palette of toppings, tart ripe tomatoes, a savory paste of capers and anchovies, sweet stewed onions, mellow, cool mozzarella and peppery arugula, accompanied by our second wine. About 40 minutes later, we moved uphill to another table and were served amazingly tender, full-flavored veal chops sautéed in balsamic vinegar, plus a third vintage.

It was only then I noticed that the stars were out; we'd been engrossed in eating and conversation. Dinner with Guido was always a business dinner in the sense that I was dining with someone I did business with, but we never talked about business, or The J. Peterman Company. We talked about life, expectations, food, travel. Guido's 92-year-old father joined the party now. I don't know if he drove himself to the restaurant, but I believe he could have; he was sharp. He'd been an agent in the business before Guido and Guido's brother, Carlo; they all spoke English and they moved between languages as easily as you'd go from a bite of bread to a sip of wine.

Finally, a weightless pastry filled with fresh whipped cream. Rosanna came by, bearing a pitcher of warm chocolate, which she poured generously over each serving; it tasted like melted Teuscher truffles. You might have called the dessert a profiterole, I suppose, but it transcended naming.

That meal lasted five hours.

I read recently in an American magazine about a movement called "Slow Food." Down with microwaves! No more eat-and-run! Do you think we have the wisdom to pull it off?

———◆———

As wonderful as Italy is, it was always Ireland that came to mind first when I felt things were getting to be too much and I was losing my edge. Any pretext for going would do.

"They say there's a knitting factory in Balbriggan run by a young witch."

"I'll check that out myself."

The Irish understand the importance of comforts better than anyone else, thick sweaters and soda bread and peat fires and sturdy Connemara ponies. Something to do with the weather, and history. They know it's a poor world that consists only of facts, and to ensure that theirs doesn't they've established a network of convenient pubs radiating from Dublin throughout the land. We ran some "Irish Pub Shirt" copy that captures the spirit:

It's Friday night at the Hog & Fool, a 200-year-old pub off O'Connell Street in Dublin.

World headquarters for conversation.

Dark mahogany walls. Lean-faced men. Ruddy-faced women.

The bursts of laughter aren't polite, but real, approaching the edge of uncontrol. The stories being told are new, freshly minted, just for you, my dear.

There is no higher honor.

If nothing else, you could justify a trip to Ireland by invoking serendipity. Many pubs, for example, double as general stores with an unpredictable variety of merchandise tucked away in a back room somewhere. Over the course of an evening in a pub near Galway I saw emerge a pound of treacle, a mousetrap, a three-barreled hunting rifle, and a side of dried bacon that resembled a violin.

I recommend a visit.

———◆———

Not too long ago, in the big picture, a trip to California from eastern Kansas, say, could take you about five months by wagon; today, if you happen to have an SR71 Blackbird at your disposal, you can make it in as little as an hour. An amazing gain in efficiency. All you give up is the chance to make a few discoveries along the way—about the world, your fellow human beings, yourself.

I've always tried to slow down the pace of travel when feasible, not by hailing a Conestoga, of course, but choosing a boat or a train instead of a jet. Helps me gain and regain perspective, and maybe pick up a few things. It was on the deck of that banana boat I hopped to Costa Rica, in my twenties, that I first consciously realized I wanted to navigate my own ship in life someday, instead of working for corporations.

When I had to get from Munich to Vienna one time, the choice was obvious: take the train and stay over a day in Mozart's hometown, Salzburg. On the second leg of the trip I found myself in a semi-private compartment, wondering if I should share the bottle of Moselle I had in my Gladstone with the white-haired gent sitting opposite. The conductor came and asked for our tickets; as I handed mine over, I unleashed my German—I'd employed a succession of plucky student tutors from the University of Kentucky to help me learn to speak the language.

"Wann kommt der Zug in Vien an?" I said, or meant to, anyway.

Incomprehension flickered between the conductor's eyebrows. "Bitte?"

I inquired a second time as to when the train would get to Vienna, pronouncing the exotic words as carefully as I could, which may have encouraged him to be more forgiving.

"Ach so! Punkt Sieben Uhr, mein Herr!"

When the conductor had left, the older gent smiled at me. "Your German is Scheisse," he said, in a Midwest accent. Turns out he was from Cedar Rapids. One thing led to another, and soon we were sharing the Moselle.

He'd been an agent with "Wild Bill" Donovan's OSS, he told me, the Office of Strategic Services, forerunner of the CIA. At the end of WWII, he traveled around Austria burying caches of small arms and gold to be retrieved later on, if the Soviets decided to push the Iron Curtain further west and a counterinsurgency was started.

They must have dug it up by now.

No, it was all still buried. He couldn't remember any exact locations, that was a long time ago, but he knew there was a map in a safe at the U.S. Embassy in Vienna.

I felt myself being sucked into a Graham Greene novel. "Fascinating," I said, and steered the conversation onto the topic of clothes.

Smart move. He gave me something almost as good as gold itself—the name of a little shop off the Kärtnerstrasse that specialized in chic, understated versions of transitional Tyrolean styles. Discovered a women's jacket there, velvety deer suede, that became one of our highest-priced long-term best-sellers.

———◆———

A young friend of mine who lives in Manhattan had saved enough for the down payment on a co-op; why make the landlord rich? He only wished that he also had enough to buy a country place for weekends and vacations.

"Take my advice," I told him, "get yourself a country place first. Contrast is everything."

I have a 550-acre farm about an hour north of Lexington, near Blue Licks, where they fought the battle that ended the Revolutionary War in the west, 10 months after the British surrendered at Yorktown. The property was run down when I bought it in 1994. The fences were rotted. The siding was coming off the barns. The machines were rusted antiques. It needed a lot of work. Still does, just to operate as a farm. One of my sons lives there; he runs the place, but I help out as often as I can.

I bring in the hay. I work the cattle. I mow the pastures for hours. We cut firewood together, build fence, do all sorts of other chores. I'm exhausted after a day on the farm, usually, but I'm renewed.

Working with physical things is a great relief from pushing words and worries around. There are no "ifs" in nature. You see results then and there, and can leave the job feeling good about yourself again. Besides, have you ever noticed how you get some of your best ideas when you're shaving or taking a shower, how it "comes to you" when you stand up from your desk and walk around? Chopping wood is very effective, too.

The farm has a lot of history, "factual romance," that I can travel through. It was once part of a larger property owned by a Confederate colonel, and there exists, on the north corner of my land, a building that served as a Civil War hospital. It's beyond repair, a shell gutted the 32 rooms it used to have. I've inspected, measured, and mapped it on days when the wind wasn't blowing too hard; I found old slave shackles in the basement.

We had a murder and a suicide in the late 1940s. The son of the man who then owned the place came home and caught his wife and his dad in bed together. He killed his dad and took his own life. Someone told me that the wife still lives in the area, just up the road. I've never seen her, or found that to be a fact. People have also said that the house is haunted. I've never seen or felt otherworldly presences, but if any house has a right to be haunted, this is it.

The farm is surrounded on three sides by the narrow Licking River, and it has a slightly elevated spine down the middle; the old family graveyard is at the bottom of the rise, divided by a stone wall, slaves buried on one side, whites on the other.

A few years ago, an adjacent piece of land overlooking my original property came up for auction. One of the interested parties was a developer who had great plans for subdivision. I entered the bidding, and the auction soon came down to me and him. I remember looking at him at one point and saying, "No way you're going to get this." I paid $70,000 more than I would have if he hadn't been there, but I have no regrets. Solitude is hard to find.

I built a cabin on that land, with a view of the entire valley. It's constructed of hand-hewn logs. The floors are 80-year-old yellow pine, salvaged from a warehouse that was being renovated. The basement walls are made of fieldstone from the farm and the creeks that run through it, a true two feet thick, not cinderblock with stone facing, and the brick on the basement floor is 200 years old, taken from a house on a friend's farm. My son and I put a tin roof on the cabin so the rain can lull you to sleep better.

I do have electricity, and eventually I'll install a furnace, probably even a phone line, but all wires are, and will be, underground. Right now, there's a woodburning stove and two efficient Rumford fireplaces. The stonework on those fireplaces is the only thing in my life so far that turned out exactly as I envisioned it. I was lucky enough to find Dwayne Justice, one of the few remaining stone masons who is a true artist. Dwayne had been in the Marine Corps, Recon, Vietnam. I was in the Corps, too, if not Vietnam, so we were both members of the club. We had rapport, and it shows.

The best times at the farm are when the sun goes down and when the sun comes up. No sounds except the peepers and the birds. An occasional moo from the cows, but they are generally contented and don't make much noise. You listen to the silence and let your mind get empty.

I ride there, too. By myself, mostly, although I have been known to discuss things with my horse.

———◆———

Visits to the farm were less frequent in early 1996, unfortunately. There were no overseas expeditions. I was busy looking for capital after our first year of real loss, but the venture capitalists who'd been sniffing around our door weren't returning phone calls now. Our bank, Nations Bank, was edgy.

I wanted to spread reassurance throughout the hierarchy there. I met with our regular account man, Craig Reese; we'd soon be back to profitability, I told him. On to Craig's boss,

Rusty Bolton, who headed the credit department, and finally, Rusty's boss, your classic unsmiling banker.

"I believe we can work our way out of this situation," I said, and meant it.

"We believe you," he said calmly. "We're not going to pull your credit line. Don't worry about that. We're stuck with each other for now."

He paused before the "for now." No mistaking his message. We'd have to find a new bank . . . as well as rethink The J. Peterman Company.

I cannot conceive of any vital
disaster happening to this vessel.

—Capt. E. J. Smith, White Star Line (1850–1912)

My Voyage
on the *Titanic*

G rand Central Station, New York, New York. Crossroads of the world. Jazz music, laughter, clink of glasses drifting out the door to the left of the main station entrance into the evening air on 42nd Street, where a stylish crowd waits in line to get in.

From atop the building, the statue of Mercury, god of commerce, presides over the opening of J. Peterman's new flagship store.

I've been inside since the breakfast tour for investors. "Freshest retail concept I've seen in ten years," said the senior analyst from Goldman Sachs. My feet are aching. Smile, I tell myself; CNN, NBC, and ABC are here, as well as all these invited customers.

There's a Catherine Deneuve type in fur hat and leather Spy Coat ("bring back the memories they erased during your debriefing") . . . two chaps in Gatsby Shirts and Niven Blazers

167

. . . older gent in a burgundy Non-Ironic Velvet Vest ("Irony is the mode of limited expectations") . . .

A woman in the Vienna Woods deer-suede jacket is standing very close to me and quoting catalog copy from memory, bright-eyed, barely audible over the room-roar:

" '. . . Tiergarten . . . pieces of chocolate . . . feeding them to a stag.' "

Nantucket Sweater has moved into position to speak with me next.

Finally, the last hors d'oeuvre has been consumed. The tuxedoed waiters have closed the wine bars. I collapse into one of our mellow old English leather club chairs. It went well, I'd say, and I wouldn't be surprised if we did $20,000 in business, too. (The actual figure proved to be $27,000.) Who on Earth could have possibly imagined two years ago that we'd be where we are today?

———◆———

Retrenchment followed our loss in 1995. The company-wide attitude was that we'd deal with problems methodically, one by one, and muddle through without selling the Holbein.

Our expenses were as high as current revenue could support. We addressed that by streamlining the way we worked, using more part-time, as-needed help in customer service and shipping and cutting back on staff in merchandising, sourcing, and product development; we'd gotten a bit fat in terms of hiring assistants.

Writers and artists were asked to take a cut for the time being, too; they grumbled, but being associated with The J. Peterman Company had cachet.

It seemed to be another soft year for the catalog industry; nothing much we could do about that. We did pull back on our mailings to new prospects, though, which helped us gain some ground.

Beyond retrenchment, there was the matter of rethinking the business. I'd finally acknowledged that our wonder years of growth as a catalog operation were behind us. Only one out of four people buys from catalogs. On the other hand, everyone shops in stores, and the fact is, we'd had a successful retail store in Lexington since 1992, along with several off-price outlets around the country to unload our excess inventory. The Lexington store was a hobby of mine; I'd kept experimenting with layouts, displays, lighting, new ways to mesh hard goods and clothing, and I'd gotten it to the point where it pleased me.

We could lift ourselves to a whole new level if we were able to roll out the store concept, somehow.

———◆———

I had met Arnie Cohen once, in 1992, when he was president of J. Crew; by industry consensus, he'd done much to refine the catalog company's all-American style and more than double its sales, leading a successful expansion into retail. I asked for the meeting; J. Crew's mailing list was working so well for us, I wanted to learn more about what they did, and why.

We spent an afternoon talking about the mail-order business. Arnie was knowledgeable, articulate, a born salesman. Lots of energy.

Arnie left J. Crew shortly after our meeting because the founder, Arthur Cinader, wouldn't give him a stake in the company. He went on to senior positions at two troubled clothing firms, London Fog and Today's Man; inevitably, per-haps, the first almost went bankrupt and the second actually did. Then, in July 1996, he called me out of the blue with a proposal: In essence, he wanted equity in J. Peterman without putting in enough money up front.

I rejected that, but Arnie made himself available as a sort of unpaid consultant—and, frankly, I welcomed it. He had good ideas, a hard-to-find combination of catalog and retail experience, and his energy buoyed me; I was worn down from years of putting out fires.

As 1996 marched on, it seemed as if we'd break even, but we were using up cash, not adding it. By early fall, it was clear that if factors remained constant, our pockets would be empty once we paid for next spring's inventory.

"Cancel the inventory," Arnie said.

I looked at him in astonishment. "How can we do that? We'll lose all our vendors."

"We had the same situation when I joined J. Crew. I went around, visited the vendors in person, canceled the orders. Some of the goods were already on the docks, ready to ship. They weren't happy, but they went along with us, and they stayed with the company. You know, John, even if you do lose a few vendors, it's better than running out of money."

I immediately bought a round-the-world ticket for a very un-Peterman trip, flying from Lexington to Los Angeles, on to Hong Kong, Bangkok, and Rome, taking the train to Florence and back, flying to Portugal, and home again in one week. I met with vendors, canceled orders, explained, cajoled, negotiated. A lot of items were just going into production, the fabric had been bought but the clothes weren't made yet. Sometimes I'd tell vendors that if they held the fabric, we'd use it later, for another product. Sometimes I compromised, buying some of the orders if they'd sell the rest. All sorts of juggling. I was on the phone for hours every night with John Rice and our inventory person, discussing progress I'd made and next steps.

The hotels I stayed in, the meals . . . a blur.

It's unusual for a company president to do such dirty work in person, but it showed the vendors that I wasn't an arrogant, faceless top manager; taking the heat proved that our relationships were important to me. We cut well over a million dollars out of inventory, which kept us going into 1997, and, no, we didn't lose a single vendor.

———◆———

Arnie's retail expertise had intrigued me; his solution to the inventory problem won my trust. I wanted him as a paid consultant now, to work on a formal retail expansion plan, and then we'd hunt for capital. Once we had the money, he'd become president and chief operating officer of the company, receiving substantial equity, mostly from me; he'd finally be a partner in a business. First, though, the board of directors, including Don, had to agree.

"We need new blood around here," Don said to me. "Arnie's credentials seem good, but I'd like to do some checking first."

"Why don't you talk with Arthur Cinader? He's tough but fair."

"I'll do that."

Don returned with a favorable report. "Cinader says, and I quote, 'If I could get Arnie Cohen back, I'd do it in a minute.' The deal's OK with me, John."

———◆———

Arnie, John Rice, and I spent the last half of December and the first six weeks of 1997 on the retail plan; I also enlisted one of my sons, Tim, who has since become CFO of USA Broadcasting. The result was audacious for a brand that made a point of exclusivity. We'd build a 70-store operation in five years, boosting sales to between $250 and $500 million, and positioning the company for a strong IPO; in the near term, sales would rise 40% by 1998.

The first two venture capitalists we pitched were outfits that Arnie was involved with on a deal the year before, BMO Nesbitt Burns Equity Partners, the venture arm of the Bank of Montreal, and J. H. Whitney, out of New York. Bill Morrow was our BMO contact, forties, smart, experienced, seemed like a good guy. The Whitney rep was a bright younger fellow. Both liked the plan, especially with Arnie's experience behind it. We quickly got down to negotiating the terms—then the process stalled. We'd take two steps forward, the Whitney rep would take us one-and-a-half steps back. I felt impatient.

We were having a meeting in Toronto, BMO's headquarters—typical corporate conference room, dark mahogany, long table, padded swivel chairs, the little setup of coffee, soda, and juices. As I listened to the Whitney rep's quibbling, I thought, "We're never going to get there with this guy as part of the deal." I went to the bathroom, and when I got back I sat down and said to him, "This isn't going to work. I don't want you to invest in my company."

He stammered an objection. "I'm sorry," I said, "it's not going to happen." I stood up, shook his hand, and Arnie and I left for the airport.

On the way, Arnie smiled at me. "That was like the scene where Al Pacino gets the gun from behind the toilet and shoots Sterling Hayden," he said.

———◆———

Bill Morrow wouldn't do the deal by himself—most venture capitalists like to have someone else to share the risk—so Arnie and I went off to find another investor. We earned several years' worth of frequent-flier miles over the next six weeks, criss-crossing the country; on a single trip to New York, we did three pitches in one day. At the same time, we were lining up a new banking partner; aside from the issue of our recent rocky finances, Nations Bank didn't want to get involved in retail expansion.

By the end of May, Brand Equity Ventures, GE Capital, and several others wanted in; the word "retail" sparked considerable interest. We selected BEV to join BMO. An attractive offer from Heller Financial stabilized our banking situation, as well. Arnie, John Rice, and I closed with the venture capitalists and the bank at the same time during a three-day marathon in Chicago, sleeping on cots at our attorney's club.

The new investors put up $11 million, buying out the old ones on our board in the process. Arnie became president and COO in July 1997. The company had been relaunched, and I felt as if a managerial mountain had been lifted off my shoulders.

———◆———

My "retail laboratory" in Lexington had started almost as a whim. A friend owned a mall where space was available; he gave me a very good deal, and I knew that if things didn't work out, he wouldn't hold me to the lease.

We put in a custom-made wooden storefront with mullion windows, like the shops on Jermyn Street in London. Pressed tin ceilings. Wood floors made of old barn siding shaved down and cut into wide boards. We had early twentieth-century armoires and tables, department-store racks and display cases from the 1930s and 1940s, and unconventional lighting, islands of soft illumination in a slightly mysterious dimness. The merchandise was a thrilling jumble of unusual apparel and hard goods. I wanted to recreate the sense of discovery I'd felt as a kid exploring my grandmother's barn, which the Owner's Manual had captured well:

It's time to go to the secret barn. *Somewhere there is one.*

And it's filled with everything.

Look . . . there under that huge pile of saddles and hats . . . it seems to be the hood of a car. Oh, no. It's the Packard. It's the 12-cylinder Packard convertible someone (Emily?) once drove across the country. The doors are locked.

. . . but inside, the car seems to be stuffed with old clocks, framed oil paintings, a leopard skin, books, boots, old brass fishing reels, stamp albums . . .

You can't take it all in. At the other end of the barn you notice a marble table, a beautiful slim-wheeled two-seat carriage, a stack of a dozen carved chairs, a leather trunk . . . it's all too much at once.

One key idea we developed was to have lots of things that might not sell much, like Hindu wedding beds and Victorian silver tea sets, but made the store an interesting place to spend more time, during which a person would buy more of other products. Mainstream retailers thought it was crazy to waste floor space on slow-moving goods, just as the "square-inchers" had thought it was crazy to have only one item on a catalog page. Nevertheless, it worked. And when we rolled out our stores, sales were as high as $800 per square foot— over twice the retail average.

———◆———

The Owner's Manual always had a warm spot for the movies, which are, after all, America's collective memory. We'd use products as pretexts to pay tribute to our favorite stars: a 1940s silk blouse evoked Ingrid Bergman; a men's black shirt, John Garfield; a bias-cut satin slip, Jean Harlow. Nubby silk ties, available in navy or red, recalled the "sincere tie" Clark Gable bought in *The Hucksters*, I believe. "We'll never know which color Gable wore; the movie was in black and white."

As early as 1990, Don had suggested that we reach out to Hollywood and get the rights to reproduce outfits worn in films like *Casablanca*; it would be a natural extension of our vintage-clothing idea. Unfortunately, no one on the Coast would take our phone calls.

Now, however, Arnie Cohen was on board.

Late in July, a merchant showed me an old brandy snifter with an etched logo; would we get into legal trouble if we copied it? I looked closer: "White Star Line," the logo said. Hmm, White Star, *Titanic* . . . wasn't James Cameron's $100-million recreation of the great maritime disaster about to steam over the horizon? It was either going to be *Heaven's Gate 2* or a box-office triumph. There might be more here than a snifter.

Arnie agreed . . . and he had the Hollywood connection. We met with the *Titanic* people at Twentieth Century Fox, acquired an astonishing array of props and costumes from them, genuine pieces of motion-picture history, many created by the same companies that supplied the original *Titanic*. . . silverware, glasses, and dinner plates, crewmen's caps, mailbags, 28-foot-long lifeboats . . . plus the rights to reproduce items like the fictional Rose Bukater's boarding outfit (definitely Edwardian), and, as part of the deal, her "Heart of the Ocean" necklace, fabricated out of solid glass. "You'll make a fortune with that," a well-tanned fellow assured us.

It wasn't long before Arnie had set up a J. Peterman office in Los Angeles. All those warehouses filled with props and costumes that the accountants wouldn't let anyone throw away . . . the studios didn't realize what treasure they had there, baking quietly under the California sun.

◆

Our original hard-goods catalog, Booty, Spoils & Plunder, was where we sold many of our limited-quantity items, such as the R71 motorcycles and House-of-Commons silver, as well as posters, knickknacks, furnishings, and furniture, much of it sophisticated, specialized, and odd. The copy was often great fun, like "Soerabaja Days," for a spread of curious Indonesian colonial and native stuff:

Hasn't anyone told you about your great-great uncle Gustavus?

Dutch East Indies. Early 1900s.

Made a fortune in rubber, lost it; went on to make a second one in quinine.

Liked to sit on the veranda in his starched pink pajamas, looking out over the plantation, watching the sun set through the sulphur fumes from the volcanoes.

When he rang a small brass bell, a trained langur monkey brought him a box of cigars and a device that enabled him to smoke two at once.

These, I believe, are some of the things he intended you to have.

People loved to read Booty as much as they did the Owner's Manual, but overall, it never really made money. We tried a second approach, Peterman's Eye, with more restockable items, and more obviously eye-catching ones, so that purchasers would hear a rewarding "Where did you get *that*?" more often. Disappointment again. Maybe our customers had only so many "Peterman dollars"? Maybe a hard-goods catalog doubled marketing costs with no hope of an equivalent sales boost?

Having large quantities of cash on hand breeds optimism, however. "Let's think this through again," Arnie said. "We can get it right."

Arnie set up a meeting in New York City with Don, me, Tom Holzfeind, and a high-powered marketing consultant; starting from there, we hammered out a strategy for a new hard-goods book that centered on J. Peterman himself, recounting his travels and offering for sale the unusual goods he found along the way. We'd done that before, of course, but only sporadically, here and there in the pages, and much of the copy wasn't even first-person. This time, it would be like a diary of his journeys. Why, we could even develop a TV program based on the approach.

———◆———

There are two theories of growth. One is that you let organizational development lag behind business growth; the danger with that is you get too much business and your company crumbles from within because you don't have the systems and staff to handle it. The other approach is to build an organization that can handle the business you expect to get; that's what our investors favored.

We didn't have enough experienced people to manage all our initiatives, especially in retail, and in-house training was out of the question; at the very least, there simply wasn't time.

"We've got to staff up at the top," Arnie said.

And so we went outside for top employees, wooing six-figure executives from companies including the Gap and Calvin Klein. Very talented people. In hindsight, I regret to say, we were moving too fast for them to assimilate our culture. They tended to fall back on their previous attitudes and ways of doing things, setting up boundaries, levels, and departments where none existed previously. Company veterans found the changes upsetting; they also resented the star status enjoyed by the newcomers and the high salaries we had to pay to lure them.

John Peterman, meanwhile, found himself increasingly distanced from those daily operations.

With Arnie at the helm, I was away most of the time on all sorts of missions, from buying trips and press interviews to scouting store locations, talking with architects and designers, and, eventually, attending store openings and media events like the *Today* show Oscar special, where Katie Couric appeared in our boarding outfit from *Titanic*. The longest stretch was an expedition to India and Southeast Asia in early 1998, very different from the journeys I'd made before . . . buying trip, trade mission, product field test, and nonstop film shoot rolled into one.

My entourage consisted of Ian Lloyd, still photographer and accomplished jazz pianist, who had done a lot of work for *National Geographic*; Gordy Waterman, video cameraman, with four Emmys to his credit; and Jimmy Williams, our talented soundman. Their job was to record every step of my adventures from Singapore and Penang to Bangkok, Rangoon, and Mandalay, including a cruise on the Irrawaddy and a ride on the Eastern & Orient Express, then on to Delhi and a grand tour of Rajasthan. The results would be used to create a TV pilot and the first editions of Peterman's Notebook, as our new hard-goods catalog came to be called.

I packed much more heavily than usual, including white dinner jacket and tie for tropical Malaysia and Burma, black jacket and tie for northern India—had to look right for the camera. Everything went into a large leather trunk I had custom-made for the trip; I kept notes on minor design flaws as they became evident along the way ("studs on bottom too big," "needs front handle"), and we later reproduced and offered it for sale.

The trunk became a featured player in the drama. In my luxurious private stateroom on the E&O, there's the trunk, occupying a central place of honor. When I led a mock camel charge on the edge of the Thar desert, Ian made sure the photos showed the trunk, strapped to the back of the rear camel.

"Could you do the camel charge again, John?" he joked. "I want a better shot of the trunk."

All my hotel stays were captured for posterity. Peterman at the Strand in Rangoon, now restored to its 1900s teak-and-marble splendor ... following in the footsteps of Graham Greene at the Oriental in Bangkok ... soaking in a magnificent oversized English bathtub at Raffles in Singapore. The crew was fearless.

One evening in Singapore, Ian took us to a favorite spot of his for dinner, the Imperial Herbal Restaurant at the Metropole Hotel, where we were greeted like old friends; he'd brought plenty of film.

"Start with the raw fish," Ian suggested. It was delicious. We proceeded slowly through the appetizer menu. Ostrich. Ants. Scorpions. "The scorpion is fresh here, very good," said Ian. Not bad at all, washed down with Tiger Beer. I was too full to try the dried lizard.

I went along with most of the suggestions Ian, Gordy, and Jimmy made—usually forgot the presence of their equipment. One exception came after I'd led the camel charge and the caravan was swaying in single file over the sand dunes. The crew roared around in an open Land Rover, shouting instructions, trying to get good shots. I put up with the noise for half an hour, then told them to drop back a mile so that I could absorb the silence of the desert. I was fulfilling my dream of being Marco Polo, and I wanted to be collected when we reached the little village where I was scheduled to attend a traditional opium ceremony.

Another time, I stopped Jimmy from concealing a mike in my jacket lapel when I was going to the U.S. Embassy in Delhi for a dinner in my honor; why risk an incident if guards frisked me at the gate? The dinner was important to me, and also to Dick Celeste, the ambassador to India. He was a champion of Indo-American trade, and The J. Peterman Company could play a significant role in promoting Indian textiles, crafts, and manufacturing. Dick and his wife, Jacqueline, had put together an impressive guest list, great contacts in Indian communications and business, including some who could supply me with product.

India's socialist, centrally planned economy was being liberalized to catch up with export-oriented "tigers" like South Korea, Taiwan, and Singapore, and the state of Rajasthan was undertaking major initiatives. I was warmly welcomed by local maharajas who've adjusted to modern financial and managerial demands, much in the same way as some enlightened members of the English aristocracy have. The Maharaja of Jodpur was kind enough to let me take a spin in his wonderfully preserved 1948 Buick, and at the twelfth-century royal game preserve in Rawla Narlai I galloped on a Mogul war horse through acres of peacocks.

As usual, the crew was there to get it all. Only rarely did I steal a moment of genuine solitude, like taking in the view from Mandalay Hill. Don't miss it. You can energize yourself for the climb with a drink of freshly pressed sugar-cane juice purchased at the bottom of the hill. The air is cool and dry at the top, or was when I was there. No clutter of development around you. The hazy, blue-green Tien Shan Mountains to the east; the broad, brown Irrawaddy sweeping along to the west; views up to 200 miles, as good as you get from the cockpit of a Cessna.

It made me feel that anything was possible.

*P*ride goeth forth on horseback
grand and gay,
But cometh back on foot,
and begs its way.

—H. W. Longfellow (1807–1882)

"Come at Once,
We Have Struck
a Berg"

Woodbury Common outlet mall is set in a beautiful valley 60 miles up the Hudson from New York City, with rolling green mountains rising to the west. It's built like a little Colonial village, but it's big business—Polo, Gucci, Brooks Brothers, J. Crew, all the brand names are in residence, and busloads of people arrive each day from Manhattan to shop until they drop.

Arnie and I were there on the sunny, warm Friday before Memorial Day for the opening of a new J. Peterman outlet store. The mood was festive; we'd done an announcement mailing, and customers were coming by, admiring the store, shopping, stopping to chat.

Around 3 P.M., I heard a chirping sound. Not a bird, Arnie's cell phone.

"Hello?"

Long pause; Arnie's eyes narrowed. "That's impossible," he said. "We can't be overdrawn by that much."

I could tell he was getting impatient, the way he did when he felt someone was wasting his time. "No, you can't bounce all those checks. There must be a mistake. I'll call you back in 15 or 20 minutes," he said sharply, and hung up.

Arnie looked at me in disbelief. "That was Beth," he said, our account rep at Heller Financial. "She's been looking through our cash-availability reports and thinks we're overdrawn. Heller's going to bounce a million dollars' worth of checks on us."

It had to be a mistake. We monitored our cash-flow situation daily, keeping our cash availability balanced with all the complex formulas the bank required. We called our accounting people, our controller, and John Rice, but everyone was off already for the long weekend. We called the guy at Heller who actually worked on the cash-availability reports with us; same story. After calling Beth back to review the situation, we tried Bill Morrow at BMO's Chicago office; he proved to be in.

"Bill, this can't be happening; our cash availability is up to the minute. We've got a blizzard of customer refunds and payments to vendors out there right now. Can you come up with a million dollars to cover us until we get things straightened out?"

"Four P.M. before a holiday? I don't think so. Tuesday, probably yes."

"Well, would you call Beth at Heller and tell her that?"

Bill agreed; he'd worked at Heller, knew the people, knew how the place operated. In a couple of hours, Beth called us again; she said she wouldn't bounce any checks over the long weekend.

First order of business on Tuesday was to have the cash-availability reports reviewed with our regular Heller contact. No, we weren't overdrawn a nickel; it all must have been some kind of unfortunate misunderstanding.

———◆———

"There is a great deal of ruin in a country," Mr. Gibbon wrote of the Roman Empire; things don't fall apart all at once. It was that way with The J. Peterman Company, although on a some-what smaller scale than Rome.

We felt optimistic at the time we got the call from Beth, and we continued to feel basically optimistic for months to come. Store openings would go ahead, the first edition of Peterman's Notebook would be completed, work would start on expanding our offices to accommodate new staff. I'd even get in a buying trip to Argentina, accompanied by a CNN crew that was doing a special on me, shopping, and bring back memories of big steaks and big red malbec wines as well as exciting new merchandise. Bulkheads failed, distress calls went unanswered, but we did all we could, and we never really gave up hope, not entirely, until the last minute.

———◆———

There was another call from Beth the following Friday, and this time the trouble was real. "We've analyzed your financials again," she said, "and we've determined that you don't have enough capital. We're not going to extend your over-advance for fall."

Our line of credit with Heller let us borrow extra money to cover the extra inventory we'd be receiving for the fourth quarter, which is just about every merchant's biggest sales period. Without the "over-advance," we'd be short on inventory and would lose a significant slice of the $25 million or so in business we expected.

There was only one thing to do. We called our investors, BMO and BEV, started talks about getting a $6-million capital infusion to meet Heller's new demand, and began looking for a new bank once more.

Who knows what really goes on in the air-conditioned executive suites of financial organizations, why decisions are made and unmade? Heller had been happy with our relationship two months earlier. Was the change in attitude since then somehow related to the unannounced departure of a top Heller executive who was a champion of our deal? Was the lackluster performance of Heller's stock since an IPO at the end of April making them overly cautious? Heller had a record of being cautious with retailers to begin with; they were well-known as the people who had questioned the creditworthiness of Saks Fifth Avenue and R. H. Macy & Co.

All I can say for sure is this: if a deal looks too good to be true, it probably is. When we linked up with Heller, the terms in their proposal were so much better than anyone else's that we couldn't turn it down. We should have X-rayed it. By offering such good terms, Heller didn't leave itself—or us—much flexibility to accommodate the inevitable bumps in the road.

———◆———

The Heller situation triggered disruption inside our company, too. The relationship between Arnie and John Rice wasn't easy; Arnie wanted to know every development, every detail, in real time, while John's approach was more like, "I'll handle the minute-to-minute stuff and update you at the end of the day." After Woodbury Common, Arnie decided he couldn't abide John as our CFO, and I reluctantly agreed he had to go. I took John aside and told him how Arnie felt.

"John, " I said, "I'm asking you to step down as CFO. Having the two of you at odds this way isn't doing the company any good."

"I can't believe you're saying this."

"I can't believe it, either. I do want you to stay on, though, as senior vice president of operations. You've always been responsible for the back end, warehousing, MIS. The move into retail means a whole separate fulfillment system. Nobody can bring that off like you."

John wasn't happy about the change. He took a few weeks to think it over, but eventually, he agreed, and we hired a new CFO.

———◆———

By early July, we had our $6 million from BMO and BEV, bank talks had been initiated, and we'd reconnected with GE Capital. GE was enthusiastic. They said they'd put in $9 million if management came up with $1 million, and we agreed we'd close by the end of the month.

We brought in a consultant from Ernst and Young to act as the point man with GE and our new banking prospects. Financial types began to show up in Lexington, doing due diligence, meeting with Arnie, me, and other managers, while the point man kept running numbers into the various formats they required. We staggered the visits so they wouldn't overlap. Each day, a different platoon of three-piece suits made its way through the hubbub of construction—hammers banging, drills whirring, workmen shouting, big sheets of plastic divider hanging down here and there—to the relative peace of a conference room. There was an upbeat energy in the air.

The mood wasn't punctured when Heller refused to OK routine waivers signed by our store landlords agreeing if anything happened to us, the bank, not the landlords, owned the inventory; the wording wasn't stringent enough anymore. While that created a problem with our landlords, it mostly underscored the urgency of what we were doing. We tried to speed up the GE deal, which dragged through the legal process past July 30, for a same-time closing with BankBoston, the firm we chose as our new banking partner.

Finally, on September 2, Arnie and I closed with GE, alone. We flew to New York for that one with our attorneys, sitting in the GE attorney's office for two days, negotiating until the moment the fountain pens came out. It sounds exciting, getting $10 million. It's not. Instead of someone showing up with a suitcase full of money, they simply wire it to your account . . . click, click, click, a few keystrokes, all done. An anticlimax to the deal-making stage, where you find yourself agreeing to terms whose ultimate consequences you're not sure of, giving up something you thought you needed or trying to bluff to gain more ground.

I left for Argentina two days later feeling pleased that the GE deal had gone through and confident that BankBoston would be sewed up when I returned two weeks later.

———◆———

I came back from Buenos Aires with wonderful finds, like crates of seltzer bottles that had seen good times at tango clubs and polo matches in the 1940s ("Let me freshen that for you, Evita"); BankBoston hadn't closed, however, and now there was trouble on the catalog front.

The first definitive mailing results for fall were in. Sales from the Owner's Manual were soft, and Peterman's Notebook sales were way below projection. After all the effort on developing a new format, the expensive book (90 cents per copy to produce versus 60 cents for the Owner's Manual) simply hadn't clicked. Between the two catalogs, we'd be off September revenue projections by $1 million.

Then the other shoe dropped: our printer went down. The second mailing of the Owner's Manual was delayed more than two weeks, throwing September revenue off an additional $1.5 million.

BankBoston adopted a wait-and-see attitude. They wanted us to have a $6-million cash cushion—which we did, at the beginning of September—but those reduced revenues, combined with the fact that Heller was still quibbling over the landlord waivers and withholding inventory financing for the new stores, meant that by mid-October we had $4 million less on hand than we'd planned.

————◆————

The opening of our San Francisco retail store in early November was costly, but we couldn't afford to pull out. The full-price stores we opened that fall (in Seattle and at Grand Central Station in New York, as well) had all been too far along the track, and besides, they were very successful. To me, they represented a future we'd get to after we dealt with our current problems.

While we were in San Francisco, Arnie received another phone call from Heller; they were going to further ratchet down our advance rate. We arranged a conference call with our board of directors. According to the financial plan we'd been reworking since early October, we faced a $6-million shortfall. This was a full-blown cash crisis.

When we returned to Lexington, the board directed us to put all our merchandise on sale for the holiday rush, which probably boosted our sales 10% but left millions in profit on the table. We also learned that BankBoston would do a deal if our investors would guarantee the $6 million we needed. The MBAs for GE, BMO, and BEV arrived at Russell Cave Road to vet the financial plan, and at the board's suggestion, we hired

Zolpho Cooper, a firm of street-smart accountants that handles bankruptcies; in our case, the idea was to keep us out of bankruptcy.

The MBAs and the Zolpho people were churning out numbers night and day in Lexington, working hard to right the ship; much time was wasted, though. They often used incomplete or inaccurate data, or they'd do analyses with the same numbers, each in a different way, and then spend a week trying to figure out why they came to different conclusions.

A variety of informal "save-the-company" ideas were being offered. One true friend of the company suggested that instead of trying to jump through hoops, we should file for bankruptcy right away; we'd get into a legal catfight with Heller, but we could keep all the money that came in until the battle was settled, and that would carry us through. It was a good plan, I realize now.

Other proposals were unrealistic or almost laughably naive. "Orient Express posters, that's the solution," someone told me. "I saw this collection of a thousand Orient Express posters in France, the real thing, from the 1920s and 1930s. We'd make a fortune selling them in the catalog."

"That's an idea," I said, "but we're not going to have another catalog to sell them in unless we solve our financial problems first."

The firing started in early December. December 7, 1998. The first round of cuts came mainly from merchandising, product development, sourcing, and marketing, the places where we'd staffed up in expectation of retail growth. By the end of the month, we'd had a second round, going deeper into the organization. Audrey set up an outplacement facility to help employees find new jobs. The local press took notice, negative notice, and the news didn't stay local for long.

All our people knew what was going on, we were open about it, but they kept working hard on product and catalogs for the spring and summer of 1999. They seemed to believe that I wouldn't allow anything to happen to the company. Perhaps, in truth, they felt differently, but I can't think of anyone in any department who wasn't supportive in what they said to me at the time.

I didn't enjoy shaving in the morning.

December 18. Heller imposes a forbearance agreement. We are on notice that they intend to terminate our relationship and will not finance purchase of further inventory.

———◆———

At the end of December, Zolpho Cooper delivered a "liquidation memorandum," which said, in essence, that if our assets were liquidated on January 1, Heller would be paid off in full and the venture capitalists would get varying amounts of their money back. The memo was intended as a useful guide for us; looked at cynically, however, it might have suggested that for some, a quick bankruptcy of The J. Peterman Company could be the safest bet.

The investors and Zolpho then approved the financial plan, basically the same one we'd had back at the start of November, and I went to Chicago to discuss next steps with Heller; with me were our attorney and reps from Zolpho and GE. In the opposite corner was Beth, plus some faces I hadn't seen before. The atmosphere was tense. At one point, Beth began to say it out loud:

"We're looking at the numbers we get from workout..."

"Workout" is where the bank takes all the money you have coming in and doesn't lend any more.

"Do you mean to say you intend to force us into bankruptcy?" I asked.

"Certainly not. We're giving your investors a week to come up with the $6 million."

The GE rep objected. "We'd need two weeks to go through legal."

"Very well, then, we'll give you ten days."

Those days went by the way they do in old movies with the shot of calendar pages tearing off and fluttering away. The investors didn't get it together in time, and Heller put us in workout. But Arnie grasped at one last straw.

"I have a friend at Bear Stearns," Arnie said.

———◆———

Arnie and I and our new CFO flew to New York for a meeting at Bear Stearns's offices. We spent all day with the investment bank's people and left at 6 P.M. with a $10-million deal that was going to save the company. It had contingencies, but it was a doable deal.

We immediately took a train out to Greenwich, Connecticut, met with BEV, and had them behind us by 10 P.M. The next day, it was up to Toronto and BMO; Bill Morrow was there. By midafternoon, they'd decided to go along with us, as well.

Bill left the room to check on messages. "OK, now the next step," I was thinking.

When Bill returned, he was frowning. "John," he said, "I got a phone mail from GE. It sounds like they're not going to go along with the deal. And if GE isn't in, we won't be, either."

We departed for the Toronto airport feeling grim. Heavy snow, the plane was delayed. I kept trying to raise the GE rep on my cell phone and finally got through.

"Hey, John, how's it going?"

"I hear you're out."

"Absolutely not. Where did you get that? We're in. We want to do this."

I called Bill, reached him at once, and told him about the conversation. He sounded wary, but agreed that if GE was in, BMO was, too.

This went on for a few days. We'd call Bear Stearns and they'd say, "Yes, but we haven't heard from GE yet." Then we'd call GE and they'd say, "Well, we called Bear Stearns, but they haven't called back."

Some deals just don't seem to want to happen. Too bad, Bear Stearns could have afforded it. They're a successful player, with a range of funds favored by institutional investors—one of their biggest clients, for example, is GE.

———◆———

Filing for Chapter 11 bankruptcy is a simple procedure. You show up at court, hand the papers to the clerk, who passes them up to the judge, and after glancing through them, the judge sets a date for your hearing. It takes 20 minutes, maybe.

When the lawyers and I appeared before the Honorable William S. Howard on January 25 to obtain protection for the company against creditors, pending a possible reorganization, we asked for and were granted February 23 as the date for hearing whatever plan we could come up with. We could have gotten more time, but if we hadn't solved our problem by then, there'd be no spring catalog, no spring product, no chance for survival.

As we came out of the filing, we were surrounded by reporters, microphones, TV cameras. The J. Peterman Company had indeed become a national fixture. We were in living rooms all over the country that night; even Tom Brokaw mentioned the events in Lexington.

The hard part of the day came in the afternoon, in the lunchroom at the company. Nearly 200 employees gathered to hear the news from me, firsthand. I stood at the front of the room and looked over their faces. Some had been with us since the beginning. Some were near retirement; where would they get jobs now? What about the young parents who had medical bills and mortgages to pay? I imagined the effects of our death rippling through the community.

I outlined the situation as unemotionally as I could. Here's where we are, here's where we might go. The one positive thing I could tell them for certain was that we'd made arrangements with our bank to keep us going on a bare-bones budget, financing salaries only, in the hope that if we could hold the company together, we'd have a better shot at finding a buyer.

Then I took the questions.

———◆———

A room at our headquarters was set up to receive prospective buyers, with products displayed so they could browse and get a feel for what we were about. Another room had all our records handy, so they could perform due diligence without wandering unsettlingly through the company halls. We heard plenty of flaky proposals over the next month, from people who often knew nothing about retail or direct marketing. The legitimate possibilities—we must have reached out to 50 of them on our own—just weren't looking to take on a troubled company at the time.

The liquidators closed in, too, drawn by the smell of assets in the water, to check out things for themselves. They'd snap us up chunk by chunk at the bankruptcy auction if we didn't find a buyer.

Arnie and I worked until 2 A.M. the day before my appearance at the bankruptcy court, trying to get a deal done with some guys from Florida, but it was no go.

Arnie never quit.

Neither did a lot of other people.

———◆———

February 23. I appeared back at court and got a date of March 5 for the bankruptcy auction. In the late afternoon, we threw a good old-fashioned Irish wake for The J. Peterman Company in our merchandising department, with plenty of beer, wine, and food for the remaining employees; I wanted at least some of our last memories together to be happy ones. After that, I began to clean out my office.

———◆———

The morning of the auction was cold and clear. I paid a farewell visit to the company, one last walk through the warehouse and offices. Every computer, desk, chair, and lamp had a numbered tag dutifully attached so the court could identify and track the assets. Then I drove to the Hyatt Regency, in whose ballroom the auction was going to take place. The room was arranged like an amphitheater, an auctioneer's podium up front, with rows of chairs around it in semicircles. The liquidators assigned themselves to the right side, other bidders took the middle, and I ended up on the left, by myself, except for my attorney. In the rear, there was a dais for the TV cameras.

About ten minutes before the proceedings were to begin, a gentleman approached me and introduced himself, along with several others in his group; he was Tom McCain, CFO of Paul Harris, from Indianapolis, and they wanted to buy the company. Our white knight had arrived, one I'd never considered; Paul Harris was practically in another business—a chain of stores that sold midprice women's knits.

"John," asked Tom, "would you be willing to come along and help us with the company?"

"Let me ask you," I replied, "does Paul Harris intend to keep it together—the stores, the catalogs, and the people?"

"Yes," he said.

"Well, I'll come along then, too."

We went into an adjacent meeting room and Tom got their CEO, Charlotte Fisher, on a conference phone. She was enthusiastic. She admired The J. Peterman Company so much. This was such a wonderful opportunity. I didn't ask her the point-blank question I'd put to Tom, but I certainly received the impression that she had the same scenario in mind.

After we hung up, Tom turned to me. "If we're successful in buying the company, will you come to Indianapolis with us this evening?"

Yes, I would.

"Good, we have a seat waiting for you on the company plane, John."

The auction began late and went on for 11 hours. First, they took bids for each element of the business separately—the mailing list, furniture, store leases, inventory, and so on, one by one; then, they accepted bids for the business as a whole. The idea is, if the best bid for the whole is higher than the sum of the best bids for the parts, the business is sold as a whole.

The first round of bidding took forever; it was like being a witness at your own autopsy. The second one was mercifully faster. Before long, the fat man with the red hair bid the $10 million, and the company went to Paul Harris.

I felt drained after the signing of the final papers at the courthouse across the street. "Tom," I said, "do you mind if I drive up to Indianapolis tomorrow? I'm knocked out."

"No problem," he said. "Monday will be time enough."

———◆———

The next day, Saturday, an unexpected call came from Tom. "John, we've been talking this over, and we'd like about 90 days to get our arms around the company. We'd like to get back to you then and discuss how you might fit in."

I was amazed, even though I should have been used to this sort of thing by now. "Tom, that's totally different from what you said yesterday."

He tried to backpedal, but I cut him off.

"Look, we both know that's not what you said. It sounds like someone has changed her mind and you've been left holding the bag."

"I'm glad you understand."

"Well, you don't have 90 days," I said. "You have two days. On Monday, I expect to know whether I'm going to be working with you or not."

"How about 30 days?"

"Two days, Tom."

Long pause. "Why don't you assume, then, that you're not going forward with the company, and we'll get back to you if things change."

I wanted to be sure. "You mean if I show up Monday, I won't have a job?"

"That's correct," he said, and we hung up.

———◆———

A team of Paul Harris employees had arrived at The J. Peterman Company just after the auction to take possession of the business, locking files, changing computer passwords, practically counting the paper clips, with scarcely a word to existing employees. But they were perhaps even more alarmed than the employees were by an unexpected arrival on March 10.

A clattering in the sky. It was Charlotte Fisher, descending in a helicopter for a surprise landing in the parking lot. Two four-door sedans pulled up, collected her and her entourage, and drove them 50 yards to the front door.

Why would a retailer with specialized midrange experience want to acquire a diversified, upscale company in the first place? Did they have any idea of how expensive the talent and inventory it takes is? Did they think they could credibly run a J. Peterman Company without a real J. Peterman? Or was Charlotte trying to give the impression that she had some marvelous new strategy to Wall Street, which watched disapprovingly as the company's stock sank from $30 to an ultimate low of $3 under her leadership? If so, it's possible to feel sympathy for the Paul Harris people about the burden she imposed on them.

After several hours in Arnie's old office, Charlotte emerged for a tour of the facilities and then inspected the downtown retail store. "This is just to immerse myself in the company," she told the local press. She said she planned to take some time before making a final decision about the future of the J. Peterman headquarters.

Two days later, it was announced that Lexington was being closed and everything would move to Indianapolis.

*Success is the ability to go
from failure to failure
without losing your enthusiasm.*

—W. Churchill (1874–1965)

Climbing Back
on the Horse

Springtime in Bluegrass Country. Dogwood shifting into overdrive. New calves testing their legs. Racing fans pressed against the rails at Keeneland again during foggy morning workouts, listening to the snorts and hoofbeats of thoroughbreds coming nearer, hoping to glimpse the next Derby winner.

The optimism of the season was lost on me.

When the roller-coaster ride of the previous months ended abruptly I felt empty, as well as bitter. My appetite was off. I was tired, but sleep didn't come easily most nights.

I spent days out at the farm, assigning myself physical tasks to keep my mind off my mind. You always have a lot to do around a farm in the spring, and the cabin was still far from completion; I was glad I'd put off so much of the work.

I had mountains of paper to go through, too. Somewhere in the foothills I came across copy that Bill McCullam wrote back in the fall for the spring 1999 Owner's Manual, which would never be printed now. One piece in particular struck me—it was for a simplified safari shirt with big, handy pockets, which we called The J. Peterman Travel Shirt; the opening seemed prophetic:

> *As my boat sank into the Zambezi I watched all my luggage float downstream over Victoria Falls. But the day wasn't a total loss.*
>
> *The trek back to the hotel gave me time to think about things. How much does a man need, really? Where, exactly, on the great scale of muchness and littleness, is the point that's neither too little nor too much?*

Yes, I certainly had things to think about.

———◆———

America had followed the collapse of The J. Peterman Company with an amazing amount of interest. From the Chapter 11 filing to the close of the Lexington office, and for months to follow, I collected hundreds of newspaper and magazine articles, mostly accurate and sympathetic enough, like this excerpt from an Associated Press story in late January:

When Peterman published his first catalogs in 1988, they were something new: consciously upscale, with color sketches of the merchandise instead of photographs and lyrical copy that invested the merchandise with a romantic, exotic history. Printed on heavy paper and dubbed an "Owner's Manual," Peterman's book of what he called "factual romance" was meant to be kept.

There were also the inevitable satires. The *New Yorker* imagined a Peterman going-out-of-business sale, with used office equipment like wastebaskets being sold in high-flown prose. In the "Doonesbury" comic strip, a character discussed the bankruptcy with a friend as they walked through falling snow: "Cold today," she said. "Sure wish I had a nice, warm duster." Lance Morrow, in *Time*, penned a mock elegy:

I felt the way I had when Gerald and Sara Murphy closed down the Villa America at Cap d'Antibes—Scott was sober and unavailable to make scenes, anyway, and Zelda was crazy. . . . All that literary ingenuity gone to sell clothes . . . and to end up bankrupt besides.

The New York Times ran a piece in early April that appeared to be a serious postmortem. It detailed Arnie's management career, from J. Crew through London Fog and Today's Man to J. Peterman, concluding that his "daring initiatives to expand or reorganize" inevitably created difficulties, at the least, and were fatal in two cases. The writer quoted Don's well-sharpened remark that Arnie was "a serial killer of companies."

That one sat on top of the pile for a couple of weeks, giving me, for a while there, a measure of cheap comfort.

———◆———

Laying down a brick floor in the basement was one of my projects at the cabin. I'd dug out about four inches of dirt, and the next step was to pour in two inches of sand to make a receptive bed for my 200-year-old recycled bricks, rolling and tamping it smooth. That meant hauling, spreading, and tamping a lot of sand.

I was glad to get a call from my son-in-law, the actor Steve Zahn, asking if he and Ethan Hawke could spend some time with me; they'd just finished a retreat at the Trappist Abbey of Gethsemani near Louisville, where Thomas Merton once presided. "Sure," I said. "I'll let you help out with something that's even more fun than whitewashing a fence."

Work went much faster with two fit and rested young fellows on the job, and thanks to their company, I could also drink more beer. The beer fueled wide-ranging conversation—

old cars, uncoursed rubble masonry, Buddhism, the Shake-speare revival, eventually settling on the topic of fame.

"Being some kind of celebrity is tricky stuff," said Ethan. "People have unrealistic expectations about you, it can distort your whole life."

I remembered our store openings, people eager to engage me, touch my sleeve, as if magic would rub off on them. "I know what you mean," I said.

"You better be secure to start with," said Steve, "or the 'public you' will make the real you feel even more worthless."

"Marilyn, Judy, pages of examples."

"The dumbest thing a guy can do is to start believing he really is what all those people think he is. Goodbye, soul."

"So what good is it, people thinking they know who you are, expecting things?"

Ethan squinted down inside the neck of his empty beer bottle. "Well," he said, "it sells tickets."

We accused each other of being famous and sentenced ourselves to another round.

———◆———

Seeing Steve and Ethan made me feel among the living, and the conversation pointed me in a positive direction. "J. Peter-man" was famous, all right, but that name had been sold at the bankruptcy auction along with our other assets. I could still call myself "John Peterman," though, just as I'd always done with the media in order to draw a distinction between myself and the company persona.

How many people out there were aware of "John Peterman"? Did they have a sense of what he stood for? I called Al Peruzzi, my friend in consumer research; could he arrange a study of "John Peterman" awareness? Al got Bruskin/Goldring's OmniTel to expedite a nationwide survey. The results arrived promptly, bound in sober Navy blue. Columns of dry statistics held good news. It turned out that the name rings a bell with 22 million Americans, including one out of three adults earning over $50,000 a year, and that "John Peterman" is recognized as a world traveler and expert shopper.

I had in my hands what Hemingway called the "one true thing," the not-always-easily-obtained seed from which a piece of writing (or in my case, a fresh enterprise) could grow.

A book would be good. And an Internet business. The Internet was hot.

Over the next months I proceeded along those two tracks (and more, really), working at an account of The J. Peterman Company, on the one hand, and a business plan, on the other. Both efforts would prove to be tentative, exploratory. But they both led me to the same unavoidable conclusion about Who Killed J. Peterman.

———◆———

Rhodes Johnston was an investigative reporter with the Anniston, Alabama, *Star* in the 1960s, at the height of the Civil Rights Movement, when little Southern newspapers that told the truth were important and dangerous. Tall, gentleman-farmer type, expert horseman, looks like William Faulkner without the mustache. I met him through his former wife, Laura Freeman, while I was advising her on marketing during the startup of Laura's Lean Beef.

(Her low-fat, organic steaks and ground beef are giving chicken and fish quite a run for the money these days.)

I drove out to the country place where Rhodes keeps his horses, to ask if he'd be willing to help me set down the story of J. Peterman's rise and fall.

"Well, I could ask you some questions," he said. "We'd record the answers, transcribe everything, then see what we've got. Of course, it won't be real unless I charge a fee."

How much would that be?

He named a not-unreasonable figure, and gave a dry smile: "Cheaper than analysis, John."

Rhodes and I held our sessions in the extension I'd added onto the back of my home in Lexington, a quiet, private room with windows on three sides that let in plenty of light and views of elm, chestnut, and apple trees. We met four or five days a week, for months, starting before 9 A.M. and going at it until around lunchtime. No phone calls, no FedEx deliveries. Just Rhodes, me, and a tape recorder sitting on the distressed-pine kitchen table between us.

"You look pissed, John. What's bothering you?"

I had serious venting to do. Bankers were a favorite topic. I recalled scenes of betrayal and humiliation. My face got hot and my voice became louder as the little details came back to me—the upturned palm, the French cuff, the raised eyebrow, the shrug. Afterwards, sometimes, I'd yawn and feel lighter.

"How'd you come across the duster—Aspen, was it?"

It was a pleasure to revisit times like that, when I had a dawning sense of promise, followed by hard work and stress, yes, but positive stress, and then a wind-in-the-hair feeling that we had the momentum and nothing could stop us. Laughter in the halls. Great press. Fan letters. Bigger offices. Trips to all the places I'd read about in *National Geographic*, up in the attic long ago.

"We're getting some terrific material now, Rhodes, don't you think?"

"We'll see."

Gradually, the questions became more probing, and persistent. Rhodes kept returning to the subject of Arnie Cohen. "You say Arnie did too much, too fast, right?" I nodded. "But you OK'd it all, didn't you?"

"Isn't that obvious? But we *did* need to expand into stores to get new customers, you know."

"Let's forget stores for now. Why did you agree to start a new catalog title and try to sell even more stuff to your current customers? You'd seen that approach fail, hadn't you, when you went along with Don's idea to put more into the Owner's Manual?"

"Arnie had won my confidence. I believed in him."

"You believed in *something*, John, and more than once. Is there a pattern here?"

I noticed a chipmunk run across the outside window sill.

Another time, Rhodes zeroed in on "The Heart of the Ocean" necklace. "That glass necklace from *Titanic*," he asked, "how did that fake get into the catalog?"

I felt like I'd been slapped. "That was a best-seller. We sold thousands of those necklaces at $198 each."

"I didn't say the necklace failed to sell, I said it was fake. You weren't in the business of selling fakes, were you?"

"Hell, no."

"Didn't you have a company policy statement hanging on the wall to remind people of what *was* Peterman and what *wasn't*?"

" 'Mission statement,' " I corrected, crossing my legs. "No . . . nothing formal. What the hell do you want me to say, Rhodes—'Guilty, Your Honor'?"

"That's good, John, very good."

I didn't laugh.

By the time we'd accumulated 1,500 pages of transcripts, I could tell where we were going. "Instructive," you might call it. It wasn't really fitting in with my practical plans as they were evolving, though, and it was taking up a lot of time. I was a bit sad as we got toward the end of what I'd decided would be our last session. I wanted to make this easy.

"Rhodes, this has been great, I mean it . . ."

He made a small "Stop" gesture. He'd known for a while this was coming.

"I'm a reporter, John. I dig for the dirt. That's not the kind of story you want to run."

We shook hands and parted friends.

———◆———

When I wasn't having marathons with Rhodes Johnston, I was usually busy shaping a business plan grounded on the "John Peterman" research that Al Peruzzi had supplied. The Internet played a key role in my thinking; if nothing else, I figured, I could get back into business faster and cheaper with a Website than through any print-catalog operation that would be appropriate to the name "Peterman."

Another happy illusion of inexperience.

The J. Peterman Company had put up a Website in 1997, but it was never more than a smattering of pages taken from our catalogs, with a shopping cart added. We'd never thought deeply about the special nature and potential of the Web. Now, I began talking to friends who'd had real experience with it, reading some of the better books on the subject (e.g., Hagel and Singer's *Net Worth*, Kelly's *New Rules for the New Economy*, Siegel's *Futurize Your Enterprise*), and drawing lots of boxes connected by straight lines.

I learned that the model *du jour* for Internet business was the information intermediary, or "infomediary," and there was a seductive simplicity to it. You built a Website that attracted consumers with some kind of heavily promoted service, entertainment, or information, collected data on their interests and demographics, then marketed the data to other businesses that wanted to target their sales efforts to customers who fit specific profiles.

Marvelous. Here was something that could spare me from my familiar bugaboo, the need to carry inventory. Inventory is always risk, and anything that's sitting unsold in your warehouse is frozen capital. I wouldn't even need a warehouse.

I plugged an infomediary module into the center of my business plan and did the math. The numbers confirmed that I had a thoroughly modern dotcom scheme: The company would lose at least $10 million over a two-year period, then go on to conquer the world, earning triple that by Year Four.

"Wait a minute," I said to myself. "Stand back. Take a look at this thing."

I might not be investing in hard inventory, but I'd still carry the burden of large startup costs. The calculated returns were just too rosy, especially in an e-commerce environment that was changing so fast and unpredictably. Those problems weren't unlike the ones we'd faced at J. Peterman, essentially. Did I really want to reinvite them, on a bigger scale?

Clutter had become a problem in our catalogs, eventually, but at least it was a clutter of items with J. Peterman labels sewn into them. Here we'd be cluttered right from the start, and with other companies' ads, banners that make sites on the information superhighway look like those crowded intersections with whirling, flashing, plastic signs for gas stations and fast-food joints. I'd always prided myself on treating customers with respect. How respectful would this be?

I also bit the bullet on the matter of inventory. I had to carry inventory. Some, at least. The research showed that people thought of "John Peterman" as a world traveler and expert shopper. They *expected* him to offer them his discoveries. Was it rational to turn my back on that core expectation?

I crumpled up the plan and started over.

I crumpled up the next plan, too.

———◆———

Early that summer there was an unexpected phone call from the *Harvard Business Review* up in Boston. An editor named

Regina Maruca. The Brahmins of business had observed the Peterman bankruptcy and thought their readers would be interested in getting the whole story. Would I be interested in writing a formal case study?

Sorry, I don't wear white shirts and ties.

Regina was persistent, however. Called back a few weeks later. Well, she asked, how about a relaxed, first-person account? That was more like it. She worked closely with me, shaping my recollections and thoughts into a piece entitled "The Rise and Fall of The J. Peterman Company." The account created a stir, prompting coverage in the general press.

I've always found that something real, even a small chunk of reality, will bring possibilities within its field of gravitation, so to speak, and help them to become real as well. That's what the *Harvard Business Review* article seemed to do. Website people and financial sources appeared on the horizon. Soon, I had a literary agent, then a publisher. I began work on this book with Regina, and later, Bill joined in.

Don had always said that if he were hit by a truck, I should call on Bill. He was right.

———◆———

Entrepreneurs are the much-sung heroes of American business. The pioneers, the experimenters, the risk-takers who (if they succeed) end up creating jobs and making life better in some way for everyone else. That's the official story, and I believe it.

As a group, they have at least three qualities in common: boundless faith in the potential of their ideas, which keeps them moving forward despite difficulties and the doubts of others; willingness to wear any hat and solve any problem within a young organization; and the ability to communicate an energizing sense of mission to those around them through their personal presence.

Those traits served me well during the launch of The J. Peterman Company and for some years after. Eventually, though, they became less relevant to its operation. In fact, what had been strengths became weaknesses. Decision by decision, action (or inaction) by action, I as chief executive made the company fatally vulnerable to a run of bad luck it might otherwise have survived.

The Greeks had a word for this: tragedy.

The experts had been wrong to dismiss our potential market as "kooky college professors"; our exciting initial success proved they were wrong. I felt vindicated. After that, I wasn't inclined to go back and take a cold, hard look at the whole concept of growth, how much we might expect, how we should try to manage or control it. My unexamined premise was that somehow, we could always grow our way out of problems—Harrison Ford could escape the giant rolling boulder by leaping up and grabbing onto an overhanging tree branch.

I was too receptive to advice that flattered that premise.

Entrepreneurs genuinely need to take on many roles in their understaffed companies, at first, from chief cook to bottle washer. It can be exhausting, but feeling indispensable is habit-forming. Insidious, really. I never consciously pulled the tricks some founders do to feed the habit, like setting managers against one another in order to play Solomon. Still, I tended to be involved in too many tasks, too much detail.

Overinvolvement sapped me of energy, perspective, and judgment at precisely the moments when they were needed the most.

Finally, in the early days, entrepreneurs are constantly in touch with everyone on their tightly knit teams. They communicate firsthand their vision of the business. It's possible to get by, then, without explicitly writing down brand character, target market, and strategy to guide thought and action. That's how it was at J. Peterman. As we grew and the pace of change speeded up, I continued to assume that new people joining us either understood our game or would catch on soon enough by osmosis.

Not true. Without written directions, they wandered. I wandered, too.

I'm still an entrepreneur in my bones. The act of creating is what drives me. But I'm a smarter kind of entrepreneur. One who has painfully gotten to know himself and can anticipate the challenges that come with success.

My next venture is in fairly sharp focus now. Here isn't the place to give details, but I can say this much: it involves building a brand thoughtfully. I still have a Website in mind, among other things, and I believe it will be wonderful, but it's not at the center of my business plan; the brand is.

———◆———

Back when there still was a J. Peterman Company in Lexington and I had breakfast in town every day, I'd sometimes see a gentleman named W. T. Young dining by himself, or trying to. He's the father of my friend, Bill Young, Jr., who runs Lexington Carting, and an authentic local legend. Sold his peanut-butter company to P&G in the 1950s (they renamed the product Jif®); went on to start other businesses, devote himself to Lexington charities and universities, breed and race about 80 stakes winners; his colt Grindstone won the 1996 Derby by a nose.

Guys would always be approaching W. T.'s table to apply the massage oil, and he was always gracious, but I never introduced myself; I figured I'd let him eat in peace.

One morning at the checkout counter I heard someone behind me say my name: "John." I turned around. Tweed jacket. Tattersall shirt. Full head of white hair atop keen, youthful features.

"Yes, Mr. Young," I said.

"I want you to know we're proud of what you're accomplishing here."

That felt much better than any award from a Chamber of Commerce.

W. T. Young recently gave the commencement speech to the Class of 2000 at Lexington's Transylvania University; he'd just stepped down as chairman of the 220-year-old school. He promised to make the shortest commencement speech in history, and his remarks got a standing ovation.

"Never give up," he said. "Never, ever give up. Never, ever, ever give up. That's all you need. Thank you."

There's only one thing that I can add to those words of wisdom:

Never give up.